hot for food

VEGAN COMFORT CLASSICS

EBURY
PRESS

hot for food

vegan comfort classics

101 RECIPES TO FEED YOUR FACE

LAUREN TOYOTA

EBURY
PRESS

contents

hey hot for food fam!

Can you believe you're holding my first cookbook?
I can barely believe it either.

For those of you new to the hot for food fam, I'm Lauren Toyota and I created hot for food a number of years ago just for fun. I didn't understand blogging, I was sceptical about the YouTube platform, and I wasn't even vegan when it all began! But now here I am with a cookbook full of hot vegan recipes and a YouTube channel with devout obsessive foodies following along every week, and I'm totally happier living this vegan life!

The original blog entries and awful WordPress template from the first incarnation of hotforfoodblog.com circa 2010 are long gone, thank god! But the passion I have for vegan food hasn't changed and has only gotten bigger since then.

After nearly a decade hosting television, I took a leap and decided to make hot for food my career in 2014. At the time I was dating John Diemer and together we were cooking up all kinds of vegan love! He was curious as to how we could make all of his favourite meaty, cheesy meals with plants, and before long he was hooked on the lifestyle. That sparked a new vision of what hot for food could be – something fun, real and comforting. We had all these ideas on how to grow the brand and get more people making vegan food (that wasn't boring). That's where producing videos came into play, and we launched a YouTube channel. Prior to 2015 we had never picked up a DSLR camera. I learned how to take pretty good food photos, and he started playing around with the video settings. One day we just made a recipe video, and the rest is history!

Making a cookbook wasn't something I had on my bucket list, honestly. Circa 2015 I even claimed in one of my YouTube Q&As that I probably, most definitely, would not ever make a hot for food cookbook. Well aren't I embarrassed! But I gotta give it up to the universe for throwing this opportunity my way. It knew something I didn't. I needed to make this cookbook, not just for me, but for you! It was something y'all kept asking me about and I could never let you down. Thanks for the nudge – I'm so thrilled to share this book with you.

What you've got in your paws is a shiny printed version of some of hot for food's most popular recipes and more than eighty more brand spankin' new ideas that will not appear anywhere else. The photos are all new too. My resistance to creating all this was just a big ol' bunch of fear, and believe me, that fear kept rearing its ugly head during the entire process of birthing this thing. But great challenge brings even greater reward. I guess the task of creating a book was so much more pressure for me than delivering YouTube videos every week. Prior to this career path I spent nearly a decade hosting and producing television, so I'm comfortable being on camera and editing video, but I certainly hadn't wrapped my head around publishing a book. A book is permanent, it lives on forever, and I can never go back and edit something. I'm also asking people to pay for it. I've been fortunate enough to give you all the recipes and content for free up until now! So I think that all got to my nerves. A few panic attacks and lots of hours of meditation later, it all came together. This truly has been one of the most rewarding, eye-opening and biggest learning experiences of my life. For that I'm beyond grateful!

why hot for food?

I honestly don't remember when, why or how I came up with the name hot for food. But I feel like it's how I've always felt. You too, I bet!

My entire day revolves around food! During breakfast I'm thinking about dinner. During dinner I'm thinking about what I'm going to make on the weekend. The only way to find solace is to manifest these thoughts as delicious recipes! If I'm taking a trip, it most definitely focuses around trying to stuff as many restaurant adventures as I can into whatever time we've got. Once I almost missed a flight home from Hawaii because I went hunting for vegan chicken wings in Waikiki! Ummm, totally worth it! They're at Downbeat Diner & Lounge by the way.

why vegan?

Because I can't stomach food any other way! But it took me a long time to realize this. I spent my teenage years as a vegetarian and my college years in a constant dilemma over whether I should go back to being vegetarian or not. Bottom line: I just felt sick and guilty every time I ate meat, dairy or eggs, but my love of food and stubborn attitude about not wanting to be a bother at the dinner table kept me stuck to old habits. Finally, in 2009 I couldn't take the stomach pains and emergency bathroom breaks any longer. I had also just watched the documentary *Food Inc.* and that led me down a path of ferocious learning. That research helped me decide once and for all that I needed to go vegan. I started blogging my transition on hotforfoodblog.com, and by 1 January, 2010, I would no longer eat animals or animal by-products. My only regret is not doing it sooner!

Also eating animals is just weird to me. We're socially conditioned to do it and have done so throughout history. But we don't have to do it, especially in this day and age.

I've always had a strong love for animals, and something always resonated deep inside me that didn't feel right when I ate meat. Plus now the issue of what to eat is so much bigger and more confusing than any of us can even grasp. Do I really need to tell you that animal agriculture is the leading cause of climate change? Our food choices matter, and whether you eat vegan all the time or most of the time, or even just occasionally, it's a step in a good direction for all of us on Earth. So that's that.

feed your face

I want you to devour this cookbook the same way you binge-watch your favourite shows: ferociously! My mission from the start has been to show the world how good vegan food is and how easy it is to indulge in all your favourite foods without feeling guilty.

I know a lot of rumours are going round that vegans can't eat deep-fried food, ice their cakes with sugary buttercream or consume fat and salt. Who would want to hang out with someone like that? Not me. I'm of the belief that as long as it's free of animal-based ingredients it's A-OK to eat it! So that includes things like gooey cakes, fried everything and salty snacks. My motto is maintain a balance of foods I should eat with foods I want to eat, and make these two things one in the same whenever possible.

Right now there are enough vegan cookbooks with healthful grain bowls, raw granola bars and sugar-free cookies. We don't need another one. So it's time someone broke the rules! You want french fries for dinner? Duh! Who doesn't? And you should be able to eat them without judgement. Besides, if it's the recipe for Loaded Fries Supreme (page 140) with The Nacho Cheese (page 205) made from carrots and potatoes. . . well that's practically a salad anyway!

Needless to say, this book isn't meant to be a meal-planning guide or an example of how to eat a balanced vegan diet. You can find that kind of stuff with a Google search. Within these pages are recipes for indulgent, delectable, gourmet vegan comfort foods that you crave. Foods that the majority think someone who's vegan couldn't eat. So to all the omnivores out there. . . anything you can eat, I can eat better AND vegan. I'm in the business of making food porn. Tasty, drool-worthy vegan creations that mimic the flavours, textures and feeling of dishes traditionally made with animal-based ingredients. Your other vegan books are just a tease; this is the real deal.

the recipes

Whether you want to take your vegan diet to places you never thought were possible or you're an omnivore looking to broaden your horizons in the kitchen, this book is totally worth devouring. I aim to inspire you to cook, love eating and feel great while doing it. Check out the collection of Badass Brunches (page 7), Oodles of Noodles (page 113) and Finger Foods (page 33) to get the ball rolling. Then graduate to The Main Event (page 137) and Sweet Things (page 167) to impress your family and friends. For simple, easy meals and sides, turn to Hearty Soups (page 70), Stacked Sandwiches (page 90) and Veggie Sides & Big Salads (page 55). There you go. . . every dish you need to love going vegan (or vegan-ish) and an arsenal of recipes that'll convince vegan naysayers that plant based IS the future of food.

The pictures alone will have you panting, but there are also detailed instructions for every recipe plus some visual step-by-steps for some of the more labour-intensive creations I want you to master. Read every word and be on the lookout for hot tips with simple ideas on transforming meals or recipe components into new things. That way you can reimagine this food again and again and nothing goes to waste! You'll start to love and appreciate leftovers like never before.

When it comes to deep-frying, just call me queen. JK! But I seriously know how to deep fry like a boss and it's something I used to be terrified of too! You'll notice a few deep-fried dishes in this book and you need not be afraid. I recently invested in a deep-fryer, which keeps things a little less messy, but it's totally not necessary. All you need is a wide heavy-based pot and a clip-on thermometer to monitor the right temperature range noted in the recipes. Use a neutral vegetable oil like sunflower or rapeseed and as long as your oil is hot enough then the water in the food will boil, evaporate and prevent oil from seeping in and sogging up your food. When you do this enough you'll notice nearly the same amount of oil you put in the pot will be left afterward so you're not ingesting a vat of oil! And yes, you can reuse it about six times. You need to cool it completely, then strain it into a glass jar or empty container. You'll always need about 5cm/2 inches of oil in the frying vessel unless you're using a deep-fryer – then it often requires more. This is why I've noted a range or approximately the amount of oil required for frying the recipes. It will vary slightly depending on the vessel. In the case of a shallow-fry, you'll use a lot less oil and you can use a cast-iron frying pan or heavy flat-bottomed pan, as is the case with the Spicy Black Bean Taquitos (page 50) or Cripsy Crabless Cakes (page 53). These are more delicate morsels, so placing them flat into less oil to fry them and flipping them halfway through will ensure a perfect result and nothing should fall apart. After a couple times you'll get the hang of deep-frying and then you might get obsessed with it and have visions of opening your own food truck!

A reminder: These recipes have been tested only the way you see them written. If you're used to substituting ingredients and are familiar with the way other flours, oils, sugars, etc., perform, then go ahead and do your thing.. but I can't promise perfect results. That's just how a cookbook works. There are many, many ways to make the same thing, but since these are my recipes I've made them the way I like food to taste with ingredients I like using.

what you need

Part of cooking well and having fun while doing it is having all the right kitchen tools on hand. It's taken me two years to accumulate pretty much everything I need, but it makes my life way less frustrating. Here's a list of the basic equipment beyond pots and pans that you'll need to use for recipes in this book.

• An **OVEN THERMOMETER** is a small device you put in your oven to show you the exact temperature. MOST ovens are not the temperature they say they are, and a thermometer can save you a lot of frustration.

• A **DEEP-FRYING THERMOMETER** is imperative for deep -frying like a pro! I specify frying temperatures and ranges, so you'll need this tool. Guessing what's going on with hot oil is dangerous territory!

• A **SLOTTED SPOON** will help remove fried stuff with ease and will allow excess oil to drip off before removing the item from the pot.

• A **PASTRY BLENDER** is the best way to blend dough for a flaky pie crust.

• A **HIGH-POWERED BLENDER** is my true love. SOMETIMES a regular blender can work too but no guarantees!

• A **FOOD PROCESSOR** is my other love, but **SOMETIMES** you can do the same thing by hand.

• A **HAND MIXER WITH BEATERS** is a cheap and useful investment that will come in handy for making whipped cream and beating butter for baking. **SOME** people have fancy stand mixers. Good for you!

• **AN IMMERSION BLENDER** isn't necessary but is very handy for blending up soup directly in the pot and for making quick vegan mayo. It's also fairly inexpensive.

• A **WAFFLE IRON** is fun, but you only need it if you want to make waffles really bad!

• **NON-STICK BAKING PAPER** is my go-to for ensuring things don't stick while baking, but it also helps crisp up certain things (like breaded cauliflower) where I find silicone mats don't. Plus paper looks good in food styling and photography, which is why I always have it on hand.

• **WIRE RACKS** are really handy for properly cooling your baked goods and deep-fried stuff.

• **SPATULAS** (of various sizes) are so handy! They help mix doughs, cake mixes and lift delicate baked goods. Use them to scrape every last drop out of pots, bowls and your blender. Spoons are for fools! Heat-resistant silicone ones are my spatula of choice.

badass brunches

If you ain't about that brunch life, don't even talk to me! Brunch is the best meal ever invented. There's a whole ritual and culture built around it, something that's lacking from the everyday breakfast, lunch, dinner routine. Brunch is like the bad boy your parents never wanted you to date. He plays by his own rules and probably rides a motorcycle. Like Ryan Gosling in pretty much every movie, and you're the one who can't decide what you want to eat! Despite never being able to decide what I want to eat at brunch, I also like it because it's a little more indulgent, and then you can lounge around all day reminiscing about the rendezvous. Savour your weekends and treat yo'self with these recipes!

but first... bacon

Starting a vegan cookbook with a spread dedicated to plant-based bacon . . . that's my style. But seriously, the foodie obsession with actual bacon is annoying. There, I said it. Get with the times.

The future of bacon is before you . . . a tangy, sweet and smoky marinade to drown endless options in. Then you can bake or fry up a ton of 'bacon-like' crispy stuff for any dish you're craving. These recipes make decent-sized batches so you'll have leftovers and in many cases enough for multiple recipes in the book. The marinade below is the base ingredient, followed by some of my favourite options.

bacon marinade

4 tablespoons low-salt tamari or soy sauce
2 tablespoons maple syrup
1 tablespoon liquid smoke
1 teaspoon smoked paprika

Combine all of the marinade ingredients together in a bowl or wide dish with a whisk or fork.

coconut bacon

150 g/5½ oz large flaked unsweetened coconut
Bacon Marinade (see above)

Preheat the oven to 180°C/350°F/Gas Mark 4.

Stir the flakes into the marinade and coat well. There shouldn't be any marinade pooling at the bottom of the bowl, as the flakes will soak it up.

Line a baking sheet with non-stick baking paper. Spread out the coconut flakes in an even layer.

Bake for 20 – 25 minutes, tossing every 5 minutes to prevent burning. When the coconut is a uniform, deep brown colour, remove the baking sheet from the oven and transfer the bacon to a plate or another baking sheet so it doesn't continue to cook. Allow it to cool completely before storing in an airtight container. The bacon will last 2 months if stored in a cool, dry place, but it never lasts that long in my house.

almond bacon

240 g/8½ oz flaked almonds

Bacon Marinade (page 9)

Preheat the oven to 180°C/350°F/Gas Mark 4.

Stir the flaked almonds into the marinade and coat well.

Line a baking sheet with non-stick baking paper. Scoop out the almonds from the marinade with a slotted spoon and spread in an even layer on the baking sheet. Reserve the excess marinade for brushing during bake time.

Bake for 25 – 35 minutes, tossing every 10 – 15 minutes to prevent burning. Watch closely as your oven temperature and bake times may vary. If the almonds are not darkening, you can brush on extra marinade halfway through baking. When the almonds are crispy, dark brown and slightly sticky, remove the baking sheet from the oven and place on a wire rack to cool. The almonds may stick together, but once they're cooled and dry you can break them up with a sharp knife and store in an airtight container. The bacon will last 2 months if stored in a cool, dry place, but it never lasts that long in my house.

tofu bacon crumbles or slices

1 (about 390 g/14 oz) block firm or extra-firm tofu

Bacon Marinade (page 9)

Preheat the oven to 220°C/425°F/Gas Mark 7.

Depending on the use for the tofu bacon, either crumble it into small pieces or thinly slice it along the short side. Marinate the tofu for 15 minutes.

Line a baking sheet with non-stick baking paper and either spread the crumbles in an even layer or lay out the slices spaced slightly apart. The tofu crumbles will have absorbed most of the marinade. For the slices you can reserve any excess marinade to brush on halfway through the bake time.

Bake for 25 – 30 minutes, flipping the tofu halfway through the bake time and brushing the slices on both sides with excess marinade. The tofu should be much darker when it's done. It might not be crispy right out of the oven, but it will get firmer as it cools.

Store in an airtight container in the fridge, and use immediately for a recipe or consume within 10 days.

mushroom bacon

1 tablespoon vegetable oil

Bacon Marinade (page 9)

115 g/4 oz shiitake mushroom caps (about 6 large caps), thinly sliced or 2 large portobello mushrooms, thinly sliced

Preheat the oven to 180°C/350°F/Gas Mark 4.

Add the vegetable oil to the marinade and combine well.

Marinate the mushrooms for 15 minutes.

Line a baking sheet with non-stick baking paper. Lay out the mushroom slices spaced slightly apart from each other. Reserve the excess marinade for brushing during bake time.

Bake for 25 – 30 minutes, flipping the slices and brushing with excess marinade halfway through the bake time. At the halfway mark, you may notice that any smaller pieces of shiitake mushrooms are already pretty crisp. Remove these pieces and place aside until the remainder is finished.

When the bacon is crisp and slightly sticky, remove from the oven and transfer to a plate or another sheet to cool completely. Store in an airtight container in the fridge, and either use immediately for a recipe or consume within 7 days.

cassava bacon

1 cassava/Yuca root
Bacon Marinade (page 9)
1 – 2 tablespoons vegetable oil, for frying

Peel the tough brown waxy skin from the cassava and discard. Your cassava root should be firm and white, not grey or mushy. That is a sign of spoilage.

Using the peeler or a mandolin, shave off thin strips of cassava about 3 cm/1¼ inches wide to resemble strip bacon.

Marinate the strips for 15 minutes.

Heat a non-stick pan over a medium-low heat with a small amount of oil. When the pan is hot, place 4 or 5 strips into the pan. Cook for 3 – 4 minutes on the first side and 2 – 3 minutes after flipped. You may need to lower the heat so the pan doesn't get too hot and burn the bacon. Once or twice while frying a batch, add a little bit of the excess marinade to help caramelize the bacon. Also add more oil to the pan before frying each batch.

Remove the fried strips from the pan and set on a plate. Placing the strips on kitchen paper isn't advised, as they will stick.

The bacon lasts up to 2 weeks stored in an airtight container at room temperature or in the fridge. Warm up leftover strips in the oven or in a pan on the hob before serving with recipes.

the big brekky

SERVES 4 – 6
PREP TIME 35 minutes
COOK TIME 45 minutes

prep ahead

Coconut Bacon (page 9)

potato hash

900 g/2 lb baby white potatoes, quartered

2 tablespoons vegetable oil

1 teaspoon paprika

1 teaspoon sea salt

½ teaspoon ground pepper

2 garlic cloves, very finely chopped

tofu scramble

1 (about 450 g/16 oz) block medium-firm tofu, crumbled

1 tablespoon vegetable oil

2 shallots, very finely chopped

2 salad onions, white and green parts, finely chopped

1 red pepper, finely chopped

2 tablespoons nutritional yeast

1 teaspoon ground turmeric

½ – 1 teaspoon sea salt

¼ teaspoon ground pepper

4 tablespoons unsweetened non-dairy milk (optional)

toppings

350 g/¼ oz stemmed and finely chopped kale leaves

450 g/1½ oz grated vegan cheese (optional)

1 avocado, stoned, peeled and sliced

125 g/4½ oz Coconut Bacon

1 tablespoon finely chopped chives

Hot sauce

This is my go-to breakfast option every weekend. It's perfect for serving a household of hungry mouths, though I have been known to devour the whole thing! Serving meals in a frying pan makes me feel warm and fuzzy inside, and somehow even makes the meal taste better.

Preheat the oven to 230°C/450°F/Gas Mark 8.

To make the potato hash, place the quartered potatoes in a pot of cold water and bring to the boil. Cook until fork-tender, approximately 8 minutes. Drain and set aside.

Meanwhile, prepare the tofu scramble. Drain the tofu and pat dry of excess moisture with a tea towel or kitchen paper. Heat a large cast-iron frying pan or ovenproof pan over a medium heat and add the vegetable oil. Add the crumbled tofu, shallots, salad onions and red pepper and sauté for 3 – 4 minutes or until the vegetables are softened and about half cooked.

Add the nutritional yeast, the turmeric, up to 1 teaspoon of the salt (adjust to your taste), and the pepper. Stir to combine and cook for another 2 minutes. At this point you can add up to 4 tablespoons of the non-dairy milk if the mixture looks too dry and cook for another minute. Remove the scramble from the pan to another dish and set aside.

To cook the potato hash, wipe out any excess scramble from the frying pan and heat over a medium heat. Add the vegetable oil, potatoes, paprika, salt and pepper and toss to coat the potatoes well.

Cook for 12 – 14 minutes, stirring only a couple of times and allowing the potato quarters to crisp on the bottom. Add the garlic and cook for 2 more minutes, lowering the heat slightly to prevent burning.

Add the scramble on top of the potatoes in the frying pan or transfer to an ovenproof casserole dish if you can't put your pan in the oven. Surround the scramble with the chopped kale and top with the grated cheese, if using.

Bake for approximately 15 minutes or until the kale looks crisp and the cheese is completely melted and slightly browned.

Top with the avocado slices, bacon and chives before serving. Add hot sauce to taste to individual servings if you like.

flaky buttermilk scones

MAKES 10 scones
PREP TIME 30 minutes
COOK TIME 10 minutes

ingredients

225 ml/8 fl oz unsweetened
soy or almond milk

1 tablespoon apple cider vinegar

2 teaspoons freshly squeezed
lemon juice

260 g/9 oz plain flour

2 teaspoons baking powder

1 teaspoon bicarbonate of soda

½ teaspoon sea salt, or 1½
teaspoons sea salt if using
coconut oil

5 tablespoons cold vegan butter
or cold solid coconut oil

Jam and vegan butter,
to serve

These are going to go faster than the free scones at Red Lobster. . . my favourite childhood restaurant. I wanted to leave them as a blank canvas so you could experiment with additions, but if you want to make them cheesy (like the ones from said restaurant), just add 2 tablespoons each of nutritional yeast and freshly chopped chives, then add as much grated vegan Cheddar as you can handle. Hollaaaa! And if you're going for a fancy dinner roll, then fold in fresh herbs like rosemary or thyme, some ground pepper, and call it a night.

Preheat the oven to 230°C/450°F/Gas Mark 8.

Combine the milk with the vinegar and lemon juice in a small bowl. Set aside for 10 minutes to curdle.

In a large bowl, combine the flour, baking powder, bicarbonate of soda and salt with a whisk or fork. (If you're making cheesy scones, add the nutritional yeast here.)

Cut the cold butter or oil into the flour mixture using a pastry blender until you have a crumb-like texture.

Create a well in the middle of the dry ingredients and pour the liquid mixture into it. (If you're adding any other extras, do it now.) Then gently fold the batter a few times until just combined. Do not overmix!

Lightly grease a baking sheet or line with non-stick baking paper.

Place the dough on a floured work surface. Lightly flour your hands and gently flatten the dough until it's approximately 20 – 25 cm/8 – 10 inches wide and 4 cm/1½ inches thick.

Lightly flour a 5 – 6 cm/2 – 2½-inch round cookie cutter and cut out as many scones as you can. Place the scones on the baking sheet.

Try not to handle the dough too much, but create another, smaller round of dough with the same thickness as before and cut out more scones until only a scrap of dough remains.

To get extra lift in your scones, lightly poke a fork a few times across the top of each scone. Bake for 10 minutes and serve slightly warm with jam or more vegan butter.

The best breakfast sandwich

MAKES 5 sandwiches
PREP TIME 20 minutes
COOK TIME 25 minutes

prep ahead

The vegan bacon
of your choice (page 9)

vegan egg

450 g/16 oz block medium-firm tofu

175 ml/16 fl oz unsweetened non-dairy milk

15 g/½ oz nutritional yeast

30 g/1 oz tapioca flour

1 teaspoon ground turmeric

1 teaspoon garlic powder

1 teaspoon onion powder

1 teaspoon sea salt

½ teaspoon ground pepper

2 tablespoons finely chopped chives

3 tablespoons vegan butter, for frying

sandwich

5 English muffins, split in half

5 tablespoons vegan butter

5 vegan Cheddar cheese slices

Vegan Bacon

2 vine tomatoes, thickly sliced

Now I know y'all get excited about fast-food breakfast sandwiches but the speedy prep always makes them look so lame! That, and they often lack quality ingredients, which makes them a total gut bomb. But now all your dreams are alive and they're layered together in this dreamy breakfast sandwich. It's so seductive you'll forget why you ever ate eggs in the first place.

To make the vegan egg, drain the tofu of excess water. Place in a high-powered blender with the non-dairy milk, nutritional yeast, tapioca flour, turmeric, garlic and onion powders, salt and pepper. Blend on high until smooth. The batter should be the consistency of a thick pancake batter. Add a bit more non-dairy milk if you need to thin it out. Stir in the chopped chives.

Heat a non-stick pan over a medium heat and add a bit of vegan butter. Let it melt and spread it around the frying surface. Pour approximately 90 ml/3 fl oz of the batter on to the pan and gently spread out to a 15 – 18 cm/6 – 7 inch circle. Cook on the first side for 4 – 5 minutes; the patty should be bubbling and look slightly cooked through and darker in colour before flipping. Flip and cook for another 4 – 5 minutes. Fold the patty in half and then in half again, so it looks like you've folded a thick crêpe, and cook for another minute on each side to make sure that the middle is thoroughly cooked. Set each folded patty aside on a plate and cover to keep warm. Butter the pan before pouring the next 90 ml/3 fl oz of batter into the pan. As you go, you might need to lower the heat or adjust cook times, as the pan will get hotter.

When you're on your last egg patty, set the oven to grill and place the English muffins on a baking sheet. Generously butter each side of the muffins and place 1 piece of cheese on each of the bottom halves. Toast under the grill for a couple of minutes until the cheese is melted and the muffins are golden brown. Watch closely so the muffins don't burn!

Place the bacon strips in the pan once the egg patties are done just to heat through. To assemble each sandwich, place an egg patty on top of the cheese, add a tomato slice and as many bacon strips as you want and finish with the top half of the muffin. The patties can be made ahead and heated through in a pan or the oven or in a microwave before serving. You can also store extra batter in the fridge for up to 4 days.

hot tip If you're a real badass, skip the English muffins and put all this stuff on the Flaky Buttermilk Scones (page 15). Next level!

baked bean tostadas

MAKES 6 tostadas
PREP TIME 25 minutes
COOK TIME 30 minutes

prep ahead

The Soured Cream (page 210)

baked beans

2 tablespoons vegetable oil

60 g/2¼ oz onion, finely chopped

1 teaspoon smoked paprika

1 teaspoon mustard powder

1 teaspoon sea salt

½ teaspoon ground pepper

450 g/1 lb cooked haricot beans, rinsed and drained

225 ml/8 fl oz water

65 g/2¼ oz brown sugar

75 g/2¾ oz maple syrup

1 tablespoon apple cider vinegar

1 tablespoon tomato purée

1 teaspoon vegan Worcestershire sauce

spring greens

1 tablespoon vegan butter or vegetable oil

1 kg/2¼ lb stemmed and finely chopped spring greens

3 garlic cloves, very finely chopped

½ teaspoon chilli powder

¼ teaspoon sea salt

¼ teaspoon ground pepper

tostadas

12 corn or flour tortillas

2 teaspoons vegetable oil, for frying

The Soured Cream

30 g/1 oz finely chopped red onion

When I was growing up, tinned baked beans were a thing in my house. My dad was obsessed. He still drives across the border to get a brand we can't find in Canada! So I had to come up with a recipe that matches the taste he's come to love. Besides, as an adult I've never ventured down the aisle to buy these things because they're laced with corn syrup and pork. No thanks! A homemade version has been a long time coming, and you can go ahead and eat these on their own or with toast, but I thought they deserved an inspired breakfast tostada to let 'em really shine!

To make the baked beans, heat the vegetable oil in a saucepan over a medium heat and sauté the onion for 3 minutes until just softened. Add the paprika, mustard powder, salt and pepper and cook for another minute.

Add the beans and the water and stir to combine. Add the remaining baked bean ingredients and bring to a simmer. Cook for 20 minutes, stirring occasionally. You can cook the beans for slightly less or more time depending on how much liquid you like in your beans.

Meanwhile, to make the spring greens, melt the butter in a large cast-iron frying pan or non-stick pan over medium heat. Sauté the greens with the garlic, chilli powder, salt and pepper for about 10 minutes until soft, wilted and dark green in colour.

Remove the greens from the pan and keep covered to stay warm while you crisp up the tortillas in the same pan. Lower the heat if the pan is too hot. Fry the tortillas in small batches in a bit of vegetable oil for 2 – 3 minutes each side until golden brown and crispy.

Assemble the tostadas with 2 tortillas per tostada. Add the warm baked beans and spring greens, and top with the soured cream and chopped red onion.

Chill any leftover baked beans for up to 4 days. You can also freeze the beans for longer storage. Thaw in the fridge overnight and heat through in a saucepan before serving.

tofu benny with hollandaise

SERVES 4
PREP TIME 20 minutes
COOK TIME 20 minutes

prep ahead

The Hollandaise Sauce
(page 218)

tofu

450 g/16 oz block medium-firm tofu

¼ teaspoon smoked paprika

¼ teaspoon sea salt

¼ teaspoon ground pepper

1 tablespoon vegetable oil

toppings

500 g/1 lb baby spinach
or stemmed and chopped kale

Sea salt and ground pepper

2 vine tomatoes, sliced

The Hollandaise Sauce

4 English muffins, split in half

4 tablespoons vegan butter

Small handful of chives,
to garnish

¼ teaspoon ground cayenne
pepper, to garnish

This popular dish from the blog has saved my ass many times whether I'm hungover or entertaining the in-laws, so I knew it had to be included in this book. Though I was an eggs Benedict superfan back in the day, I haven't ever fantasized about the traditional version since creating this masterpiece. Give tofu a real chance if you haven't yet. It comes in many textures, and all it requires is proper seasoning and cooking technique! If you thought your vegan life would never let you dive deep into a plate full of bennies again. . . you're welcome!

Drain the tofu and pat dry of excess moisture with a tea towel or kitchen paper. Slice the tofu into quarters and slice each quarter in half lengthways, so you have 8 thick medallions.

Season the tofu on all sides with the paprika, salt and pepper.

Heat a large cast-iron frying pan or non-stick pan over a medium-high heat and coat the base with a thin layer of vegetable oil. Place the pieces of tofu in the pan and fry for about 3 minutes on the first side. Flip and fry for a further 3 minutes. The tofu should develop a nice golden crust. Continue turning the pieces to fry all sides.

Remove the tofu to a dish, cover to stay warm and set aside.

Lower the heat to medium and sauté the spinach with a pinch each of salt and pepper until just wilted and cooked through. Remove the greens from the pan. Then fry up the tomato slices for 1 minute each side.

Warm up the hollandaise sauce and toast, and butter the English muffins.

Top each muffin half with greens, a tomato slice, a piece of tofu and a dollop of warm hollandaise. Garnish with the chives and a sprinkle of ground cayenne pepper.

hot tip Here's another dish where you can skip the English muffins and go beyond with layering everything on Flaky Buttermilk Scones (page 15). Just sayin'!

mushroom & leek quiche

SERVES 6 – 8
PREP TIME 1 hour
COOK TIME 55 minutes

prep ahead

The Parm (page 207)

The Red Pepper Relish
(page 212)

pastry

250 g/9 oz plain flour

1 tablespoon sugar

½ teaspoon sea salt

225 g/8 oz cold vegan butter,
cubed

125 ml/4 fl oz ice-cold water

filling

1 vegan chicken-flavoured
bouillon cube dissolved in
225 ml/8 fl oz hot water, or
225 ml/8 fl oz low-salt
vegetable stock

110 g/4 oz thinly sliced leeks

120 g/4¼ oz sliced chestnut
mushrooms (about 140 g/5 oz)

100 g/3½ oz diced asparagus
(2.5 cm/1 inch pieces)

1 tablespoon olive oil

1 shallot, finely chopped

1 garlic clove, very finely
chopped

½ – 1 teaspoon sea salt

½ teaspoon ground pepper

1 tablespoon finely chopped
sage

1 tablespoon finely chopped
tarragon

1 (450 g/16 oz) block medium-
firm tofu

If I'm out to prove you don't need to eat eggs for breakfast, then I better re-create a dish that's essentially all eggs. You can customize this quiche to your liking by using substitutions for any of the veggies – try spinach, green pepper or caramelized onions. Just be sure you cook the veg before adding it to the filling. The Red Pepper Relish (page 212) is what makes this quiche taste nostalgic for me though. My dad would always have chilli relish at breakfast with our scrambled eggs, so it's the only thing I know, and it's essential!

To make the pastry, combine the flour, sugar and salt in a large bowl. Cut in the cubed butter with a pastry blender until a crumb-like texture is formed with small pea-sized pieces of butter throughout. Create a well in the centre of the mixture and pour in the water. I fill a cup with ice and water to ensure that the water is very cold. Just make sure you don't get ice cubes in the pastry. Fold the pastry together a few times with a spatula until just mixed but still crumbly. Do not overmix the pastry! (For step-by-step photos, see page 195).

Portion half of the pastry on a large piece of plastic film. Lift the sides of the plastic over the pastry to bring it together and gently form a ball. Finish wrapping the pastry in the plastic and gently flatten into a thick disc. Do the same with the other half. Chill the pastry for at least 15 minutes before rolling out. You can also leave it up to 24 hours in the fridge, but it may need to stand at room temperature for 5 minutes to soften slightly before rolling out. You only need one portion for the quiche, so you can save the other half for another recipe, or roll it out as instructed, place it in a tart tin, and freeze it for later. Bake the case, without thawing, as directed below.

Have ready a 23 cm/9 inch tart tin. Flour the work surface, your hands, and a rolling pin and roll out one portion of the pastry to a round 3 – 4.75 mm/⅛– ³⁄₁₆ inch thick, stopping every couple of rolls to make sure the pastry isn't sticking. Gently lift the pastry and lightly flour underneath as you go.

CONTINUED

10 g/¼ oz nutritional yeast

40 g/1½ oz chickpea flour

1 tablespoon white wine vinegar

1 tablespoon freshly squeezed lemon juice

1 tablespoon cornflour

1 teaspoon mustard powder

½ teaspoon ground turmeric

½ teaspoon smoked paprika

toppings

1 tablespoon The Parm

The Red Pepper Relish

The pastry should be at least 7.5 cm/3 inches wider than your tart tin all around. Roll the pastry over the floured rolling pin, transfer it to the tart tin and roll it over the top of the pan. Gently press the pastry into the base and sides of the tin. Trim the excess evenly, leaving 5 mm/¼ inch to work with around the edge. Fold the excess up on to the rim of the tin and gently pinch evenly all around the circumference to create a bevelled edge. Prick the base and sides of the pastry with a fork. Freeze for 15 minutes.

Preheat the oven to 220°C/425°F/Gas Mark 7.

Cut a square of non-stick baking paper larger than the tart tin so it covers the sides. Fill about halfway to the top edge of the tin with any kind of dried bean. Bake for 12 minutes. Remove the baking paper and beans and bake for a further 2 – 3 minutes until the edges are just turning golden brown. Remove the case from the oven, leaving it in the tart tin to cool on a wire rack. Turn the oven temperature down to 180°C/350°F/Gas Mark 4.

While the pastry case is baking, make the filling. If using vegetable stock, you might need to add up to 1 teaspoon salt, as the bouillon tends to be saltier. In a large pan over a medium heat, sauté the leeks (reserving 2 tablespoons for the topping), mushrooms and asparagus in the olive oil for 3 minutes until the greens are brighter and about half cooked. Add the shallot, garlic, salt and pepper, stir to combine and cook for a further 2 minutes.

Add the sage and tarragon and cook for another minute, then turn off the heat.

Drain the tofu and pat dry of excess moisture with a tea towel or kitchen paper. In a bowl, mash the tofu with a fork so it's well crumbled and combine with the remaining ingredients until all the tofu is well coated. Fold in the sautéed veggies and the stock and stir to combine well.

Spread the filling in an even layer in the pastry case. Top with the 2 tablespoons reserved sliced leeks and The Parm.

Bake for 40 minutes. The top should have a golden brown crust, and a cocktail stick inserted in the centre should come out mostly clean.

Allow the quiche to cool for at least 20 minutes before slicing and serving. It should be warm but not piping hot. Top servings with the relish. Chill any leftovers for up to 5 days.

pile o' waffles

MAKES 4 or 5 waffles
(recipe easily doubled)
PREP TIME 25 minutes, plus
chilling coconut milk overnight
COOK TIME 25 minutes

waffles

2 tablespoons ground flaxseed

6 tablespoons water

260 g/9 oz wholemeal flour

2 tablespoons granulated sugar

1 teaspoon baking powder

½ teaspoon ground cinnamon

½ teaspoon sea salt

350 ml/12 fl oz non-dairy milk

berry syrup

200 g/7 oz fresh or frozen
mixed berries

75 g/2¾ oz maple syrup

whipped cream

2 (400 ml/14 fl oz) cans full-fat
coconut milk, chilled overnight

2 tablespoons maple syrup

½ teaspoon ground cinnamon

A waffle iron is truly a brunch game changer, and it doesn't have to be an expensive investment. If you want to indulge in these wholemeal waffles or perhaps a potato waffle of some kind, any bargain you come across will get the job done. If you're looking to be efficient, you can pile up these bad boys, freeze 'em and then pop 'em in a toaster or back in the waffle iron for reheating. You can also incorporate additions into the batter, like berries, bananas, vegan chocolate chips or toasted nuts. For the whipped cream, I recommend using a chilled glass bowl and hand mixer.

To make the waffles, combine the flaxseed and water together in a large bowl and set aside to thicken for 10 minutes while you preheat the waffle iron. Place a baking sheet in the oven and preheat to 93°C/200°F/lowest possible Gas Mark to keep the waffles warm.

Once the flax mixture has thickened, add the flour, sugar, baking powder, cinnamon, salt and non-dairy milk and fold until just combined. Be careful not to overmix the batter.

Lightly oil the waffle iron and add approximately 125 ml/4 fl oz batter per waffle. Cook for 7 – 8 minutes. The time may vary depending on the make of your waffle iron. Transfer the finished waffles to the baking sheet in the oven.

Meanwhile, to make the berry syrup, heat up the berries and maple syrup in a saucepan over a medium-low heat for 5 – 10 minutes until the berries are soft and warmed through.

Scoop the thick cream off the top of the cans of coconut milk and place in the bowl. Beat until smooth and fluffy. Fold in maple syrup and cinnamon.

Serve the waffles warm and top with the berry syrup and whipped cream.

If freezing the waffles, leave to cool completely. Layer them between non-stick baking paper in a container or freezer bag, and consume within 1 month.

hot tip Buy cans of coconut cream that only contain the thick cream if you can, but if you use cans of full-fat coconut milk save the coconut water for sauces and smoothies. You can freeze it for later use!

french toast coffee cake

SERVES 8 – 10

PREP TIME 35 minutes, plus
chilling coconut milk overnight

COOK TIME 35 minutes

french toast

225 ml/8 fl oz non-dairy milk

65 g/2¼ brown sugar

30 g/1 oz chickpea flour

2 tablespoons nutritional yeast

2 tablespoons vegan butter,
melted

1 teaspoon ground cinnamon

¼ teaspoon sea salt

360 g/12¾ oz cubed bread

cake mix

1 tablespoon ground flaxseed

3 tablespoons water

90 ml/3 fl oz non-dairy milk

65 g/2¼ oz brown sugar

30 g/1 oz chickpea flour

2 tablespoons vegan butter,
melted

1 tablespoon wholemeal
or plain flour

topping

65 g/2¼ oz brown Muscavado
sugar

35 g/1¼ oz wholemeal or plain
flour

35 g/1¼ oz pecans, finely
chopped

½ teaspoon ground cinnamon

2 tablespoons cold vegan butter,
cubed

coffee-infused cream

2 (400 ml/14 fl oz) cans full-fat
coconut milk, chilled overnight

2 tablespoons maple syrup

½ teaspoon instant coffee
granules

Cake for breakfast. . . #goals! So have your cake and French toast all rolled into a breakfasty slice and devour it in the morning with a cup of coffee. Just pinch yourself to know you're not dreaming! I use a 23 cm/9 inch springform tin so the cake can be removed easily, but if you don't have one, use a regular cake tin.

Preheat the oven to 180°C/350°F/Gas Mark 4.

To make the French toast, combine the milk, sugar, flour, nutritional yeast, butter, cinnamon and salt together in a large bowl. Add the cubed bread and allow it to soak.

Meanwhile, to make the cake mixture, combine all the ingredients together in another bowl.

To make the topping, combine the sugar, flour, pecans and cinnamon together in another bowl. Add the butter and pinch the ingredients together until you have a crumb-like texture.

Lightly grease a 23 cm/9 inch springform tin or cake tin. Press the soaked bread into the tin so it fills the tin to the edges and is well pressed together. Pour the cake mix evenly over the top, filling in the gaps between the bread. Spread the topping evenly on top.

Bake for 35 minutes or until a cocktail stick inserted in the centre comes out clean. Leave the cake to cool for 15 – 20 minutes before removing the sides of the tin and lifting the cake off the bottom. If you've used a regular cake tin, your cake may come out clean and easily, or you can slice and serve the cake from the tin.

While the cake is cooling, make the coffee-infused cream. Scoop the thick cream off the top of the cans of coconut milk and place in a large chilled glass bowl. Beat with a mixer until fluffy and smooth. Fold in the maple syrup and insant coffee until combined.

Serve the cake slightly warm. Slice the cake and top each serving with the cream.

pumpkin spice pancakes

MAKES 10 pancakes
PREP TIME 20 minutes
COOK TIME 15 – 20 minutes

ingredients

130 g/4½ oz plain flour

65 g/2¼ oz wholemeal flour

½ teaspoon baking powder

½ teaspoon sea salt

½ teaspoon ground cinnamon

¼ teaspoon ground nutmeg

¼ teaspoon ground allspice

¼ teaspoon ground ginger

115 g/4 oz pure pumpkin purée

2 tablespoons maple syrup, plus extra to serve

350 – 475 ml/12 – 16 fl oz non-dairy milk

2 – 3 tablespoons vegan butter, for frying

Despite what the Internet tells me, my tastes aren't basic. I just love pumpkin spice, and I'm not ashamed. What I am is sick of all those memes giving it a bad reputation. Pumpkin spice combines all the best flavours, it works with just about anything sweet or savoury, and if you make your own, you don't have to wait until autumn to have your fix. This simple pancake batter marries real pumpkin purée with all its spicy sister wives – cinnamon, nutmeg, allspice and ginger. I'd totally name my cats after those spices.

Heat a non-stick pan or stovetop griddle pan over a medium-low heat and preheat the oven to 90°C/200°F/lowest possible Gas Mark. You'll place the pancakes on a baking sheet or plate in the oven to keep them warm while you cook.

In a bowl, combine the flours, baking powder, salt and spices together with a whisk or fork. Add the pumpkin purée and maple syrup. Start by adding 350 ml/12 fl oz of the non-dairy milk and stir together until the batter is well combined. It should be the consistency of a smoothie. You can thin it out a little more with milk if you prefer thinner pancakes.

Lightly butter the pan or grill pan with vegan butter. Scoop out approximately 60 ml/2 fl oz batter for each pancake. Once the batter starts to bubble all around the pancake and the edges are slightly cooked through, then flip. Cook for approximately 2 – 3 minutes on each side. Be sure to adjust the heat as you go, as the pan will get really hot halfway through. Keep the cooked pancakes warm in the oven until all are ready.

Serve with more vegan butter and maple syrup!

finger foods

These finger lickin' good recipes keep it dirty and are meant to be devoured one bite at a time, no plates or forks necessary. If you're looking for appetizers to kick off a party or satisfy halftime grumbles, start here. You could also sit down on the sofa and demolish one of these dishes all to yourself too – I ain't judging! And enough of these together makes a great grazing meal for a crowd.

hot buffalo chicken dip

SERVES 6 – 8
PREP TIME 30 minutes
COOK TIME 35 minutes

ingredients

385 g/13½ oz TVP pieces

1 (450 g/ 16 oz) block medium-firm tofu

2 onions, finely diced

3 garlic cloves, very finely chopped

2 tablespoons vegetable oil

350 g/12 oz vegan cream cheese

2 tablespoons nutritional yeast

2 tablespoons finely chopped chives

1 teaspoon chopped fresh dill

1 teaspoon apple cider vinegar

¾ teaspoon sea salt

½ teaspoon ground pepper

1 teaspoon chipotle chilli powder

175 ml/6 fl oz buffalo-style hot sauce

90 g/3¼ oz grated vegan mozzarella or Cheddar

Vegetables, corn chips, crackers or toasted bread of your choice, to serve

This is American comfort food at its best, and it's a dip that y'all have requested over and over again. I wasn't ignoring you, just saving it. It's creamy, hot, cheesy and buffalo-y (I promise that's a real word. . . but don't look it up). It's also the perfect dip for any rager you're throwing or an excuse to pretend you care about the football! I wanted to offer up textured vegetable protein (TVP) as a different option for vegan chicken that works well in this dip. If you're wondering, it is a soya flour product that has more protein than meat, so don't worry about where vegans get their protein, bro. But feel free to use your favourite meatless chicken product in place of this.

Preheat the oven to 180°C/350°F/Gas Mark 4.

Soak the TVP in a bowl of tepid water for 10 minutes until spongy and doubled in size. Drain and squeeze out the excess water thoroughly through a sieve.

Meanwhile, drain the excess water from the tofu and pat dry with a tea towel or kitchen paper. Crumble the tofu. You will need 150 g/51½ oz. The tofu doesn't need to be completely pressed or dry.

In a cast-iron frying or ovenproof pan, sauté the onions and garlic over a medium heat in 1 tablespoon of the vegetable oil for approximately 6 minutes until soft, translucent and slightly golden. Lower the heat if necessary to prevent the garlic from burning.

Add the sautéed onions and garlic to a food processor along with the crumbled tofu, cream cheese, nutritional yeast, chives, dill and vinegar. Season with ½ teaspoon of the salt and ¼ teaspoon of the pepper. Process until smooth.

In the same pan you used for the onions and garlic, brown the TVP pieces in the remaining 1 tablespoon of vegetable oil over a medium heat for 3 minutes. Add ½ teaspoon of the chipotle chilli powder and the remaining ¼ teaspoon each salt and pepper. Sauté for a further 1 – 2 minutes until golden brown. Stir in the hot sauce and cook for another 4 – 5 minutes to make sure all the pieces are well coated in sauce. Turn off the heat.

CONTINUED

Fold the mixture from the food processor into the saucy TVP pieces in the pan. If the pan is ovenproof, you can bake and serve the dip in this, or transfer the mixture to a baking dish. Top with the cheese and sprinkle the remaining ½ teaspoon chipotle chilli powder on top.

Bake for approximately 15 minutes. If the top is not browned to your liking, you can place the pan under the grill for a couple of minutes. Watch it closely so the dip doesn't burn. Serve the dip warm from the oven with veggies, corn chips, crackers or toasted bread of your choice. Chill leftovers for up to 4 days. Reheat in the oven or microwave before serving.

herb-loaded sausage rolls

MAKES 40 pieces
PREP TIME 50 minutes
COOK TIME 25 minutes

prep ahead

The Maple-mustard Dip
(page 210)

ingredients

1 onion, sliced

120 g/4¼ oz chestnut
mushrooms, sliced

2 garlic cloves,
roughly chopped

2 tablespoons olive oil

1 teaspoon fennel seeds

1 teaspoon dried or fresh
thyme leaves

½ teaspoon dried oregano

½ teaspoon dried sage

135 g/4¾ oz stemmed and
roughly chopped kale

100 g/3½ oz cooked or canned
haricot beans or white kidney
beans, rinsed and drained

2 teaspoons sea salt

1 teaspoon ground pepper

2 tablespoons nutritional yeast

70 g/2½ oz vital wheat gluten
flour

90 ml/3 fl oz low-salt vegetable
stock

15 g/½ packet fresh flat-leaf
parsley

1 packet (450g/1 lb) frozen
vegan puff pastry, thawed in
the fridge

350 g/1¼ oz plain flour, for
rolling out pastry

2 tablespoons vegan butter,
melted

The Maple-mustard Dip,
to serve

WARNING: This recipe is pure gluten. There's gluten in the filling and gluten in the pastry. These might as well be called gluten rolls. Sorry, not sorry! They're freakin' tasty and were inspired by those little party appetizers you buy in a box. I can easily throw back twenty of these, no sweat, and I don't feel bad about it either 'cause there's also kale in them rolls.

In a large filling pan, sauté the onion, mushrooms and garlic in the olive oil over a medium heat for 4 – 5 minutes until the mushrooms are soft and lightly browned. Add the fennel seeds, thyme, oregano and sage and stir occasionally for a futher 3 – 4 minutes until the mixture is browned and cooked through. Toss in the kale during the last couple of minutes of cooking so the kale wilts but does not overcook. It should still appear bright green.

Add this mixture to a food processor with the beans, salt, pepper, nutritional yeast, vital wheat gluten, stock and parsley. Process until the mixture comes together to form a ball of dough. It should be sticky and elastic to the touch. That indicates the gluten has activated and your mixture will be chewy in texture, sort of like sausage, when it's cooked in the puff pastry.

Some pre-made puff pastry is already rolled out thin and ready to use; others may need to be rolled out. Either way, place the pastry on a lightly floured surface. Roll as much as necessary with a floured rolling pin. Stop to check under the pastry and lightly flour again so it doesn't stick. You need a rectangle approximately 50 cm x 20 cm/25 inches x 8 inches and 3mm/⅛ inch thick.

Cut the pastry across the 20 cm/8 inch side into 5 strips approximately 12 – 13 cm/4½ – 5 inches wide and 20 cm/8 inches long. Form the filling in a log shape lengthways on each strip of puff pastry. Fold the pastry over the mixture to form a roll 2.5 – 3 cm/1 – 1¼ inches in diameter, using the overlap to seal the edge. Place the roll seam side down and slice crossways into eight 2.5 cm/1 inch pieces.

CONTINUED

Line a baking sheet with non-stick baking paper and arrange the rolls on the sheet spaced 2.5 cm/1 inch apart. Chill in the fridge or freezer for 15 minutes before baking. At this point, you could also lightly flour the rolls, place between layers of non-stick baking paper in a container or freezer bag, and freeze for later use.

Preheat the oven to 220°C/425°F/Gas Mark 7.

Just before baking the rolls, brush the tops with the melted vegan butter. Bake for 14 – 16 minutes or until puffed, flaky and golden in colour. If baking frozen rolls, brush the tops with butter and bake for about 20 minutes. Serve warm with the dip.

cheesy pesto bread twists

MAKES 12 large or 24 small pieces
PREP TIME 40 minutes, plus up to
1 hour for proofing
COOK TIME 20 minutes

prep ahead

That Dough (page 168)
The Parm (page 207)

pesto

125 g/4½ oz The Parm
70 g/2½ oz fresh basil leaves
2 tablespoons freshly squeezed
lemon juice
2 garlic cloves
¼ teaspoon ground pepper
4 tablespoons olive oil

bread twists

That Dough
4 tablespoons The Parm
2 teaspoons olive oil

I'm a junkie for pesto and obviously dough as well, so this is the best arrangement ever! I've twisted a simple pesto into That Dough, which you can learn all about on page 168. Ya that dough! You'll be a master baker in no time. I believe in you. But I'm warning you: these are extremely addictive and the kind of thing that will certainly ruin your dinner. I'm sure you're okay with that since you're an adult after all!

To make the pesto, combine The Parm, basil, lemon juice, garlic and pepper in a food processor. Once it's running, drizzle in the olive oil and continue processing until smooth.

To make the bread twists, lightly flour a work surface and a rolling pin. Roll out the dough to a rectangle approximately 43 x 30 cm/ 17 x 12 inches.

Spread the pesto on the dough out to the edges and sprinkle with The Parm.

Line 2 baking sheets with non-stick baking paper.

Fold the dough in half lengthways. If you want shorter twists, cut the folded rectangle in half lengthways. Cut the dough crossways into strips approximately 4 cm/1½ inches wide. You should have 12 long strips or 24 short strips.

Hold each strip at either end and twist the ends in opposite directions a few times, revealing the layers of dough and pesto. Place the twists on the baking sheets spaced 4 cm/1½ inches apart.

Brush the twists with the olive oil.

Cover the baking sheets with plastic film and a damp tea towel and allow the twists to rise in a warm, dark place until double in size. This could take 20 minutes to 1 hour depending on your environment.

When ready to bake, preheat the oven to 190°C/375°F/Gas Mark 5.

Bake the twists for 20 minutes until golden brown.

The twists are best served immediately, while warm. You can freeze baked leftovers, once they are completely cooled, between layers of non-stick baking paper. Use within 1 month. Warm the frozen twists in a 180°C/350°F/Gas Mark 4 oven for approximately 10 minutes.

courgette-onion bhaji

MAKES 12 pieces
PREP TIME 45 minutes
COOK TIME 10 minutes

prep ahead

The Soured Cream (page 210)

ingredients

1 large courgette spiralized or grated

2¼ teaspoons sea salt

1 – 1.4 litres/1¾– 2½ pints vegetable oil, for frying

2 onions, halved and thinly sliced

½ teaspoon ground cumin

½ teaspoon paprika

½teaspoon garam masala

¼ teaspoon chilli powder

¼ teaspoon ground pepper

155 g/5½ oz chickpea flour

1 teaspoon baking powder

4 tablespoons unsweetened non-dairy milk

1 tablespoon freshly squeezed lemon juice

Coriander leaves (optional), to garnish

The Soured Cream

I have very fond memories of eating *bhajis*, which are delightful Indian snacks. I can get them at some of my favourite restaurants in Toronto – some Indian, some Thai and at one time even a vegan British pub that has since closed. RIP Porter House. Essentially a *bhaji* is a fritter or sometimes is also called *pakora*, but I gotta stick to *bhaji* for nostalgia's sake! The ones I've had all have a base of onion and mixed in are different veggies from squash to aubergine, but the common denominator was that they were all magically delicious! I love them dipped into The Soured Cream (page 210), and I hope you enjoy sinking your teeth into these savoury little guys as much as I do.

Place the courgette in a bowl with 2 teaspoons of the salt and toss with your hands to coat well. Leave to stand for 30 minutes. Rinse the courgette and squeeze out excess water through a sieve. Pat dry with kitchen paper.

Heat the vegetable oil in a large heavy-based pot or fryer to a temperature of 180°C – 190°C/350°F – 375°F on a deep-frying thermometer. The amount of oil may vary depending on the size of your vessel.

Add the courgette to a large bowl with the sliced onions, remaining ¼ teaspoon salt, spices, chickpea flour, baking powder, non-dairy milk, and lemon juice. Toss by hand, making sure the courgette and onion are well coated.

Grab a small handful of the mixture (approximately 4 tablespoons) and gently place in the hot oil. Cook in small batches for 2 – 2½ minutes until deep golden brown. Remove with a slotted spoon on to kitchen paper to absorb excess oil. Garnish with the coriander and serve immediately with soured cream for dipping.

baked jalapeño poppers

SERVES 4 – 6
PREP TIME 40 minutes
COOK TIME 20 minutes

prep ahead

Tofu Bacon Crumbles (page 10)

The Sun-dried Tomato Aioli
(page 226)

ingredients

250 g/8 oz vegan cream cheese,
preferably flavoured with herbs,
chives or garlic

3 tablespoons finely chopped
chives

2 tablespoons finely chopped
coriander (optional)

1 garlic clove, very finely
chopped

125 g/4½ oz Tofu Bacon

7 – 10 jalapeño chilli peppers
(depending on size)

30 g/1 oz breadcrumbs

½ teaspoon smoked paprika
or chilli powder

½ teaspoon garlic powder

½ teaspoon sea salt

Vegetable oil spray, for coating

The Sun-dried Tomato Aioli

A classic appetizer shouldn't be messed with too much so I kept these poppers pretty true to what you're used to, stuffing them with an herby cream cheese filling and bacon bits. They're just the right size to eat in one or two bites with your hands. If you're afraid of being eaten alive by the heat of a jalapeño, the key is cleaning out the middle seeds entirely, but as someone who walks on the mild side I find the cream cheese and The Sun-dried Tomato Aioli also helps soothe the heat while you eat!

Preheat the oven to 190°C/375°F/Gas Mark 5.

Mix the cream cheese together with the chives, coriander, garlic and bacon crumbles in a bowl. Chill while you prepare the jalapeños.

Cut the jalapeños in half lengthways and gently scoop out the flesh and seeds with a small spoon or pairing knife, being sure not to break the chillies.

Combine the breadcrumbs with the paprika, garlic powder and salt in a shallow dish.

Line a baking sheet with non-stick baking paper.

Stuff the jalapeño halves with the cream cheese mixture. Have some of the mixture slightly piling out of the halves but not overflowing. Sprinkle the tops with the breadcrumb mixture, coating them well. Place on the baking sheet.

To help brown the tops, spray with a light coating of oil. Bake for 18 – 20 minutes until golden brown.

Serve immediately with a drizzle of the aioli on each piece or serve the aioli on the side as a dip.

southern fried cauliflower

SERVES 4 – 6
PREP TIME 25 minutes
COOK TIME 75 minutes

prep ahead

The Spicy Sriracha Aioli
(page 227)

cauliflower

600 – 675 g/1 lb 5 oz –
1 lb 9 oz cauliflower florets
(two-bite size)

2 tablespoons vegetable oil,
plus 1 – 1.4 litres/1¾ – 2½ pints
for deep-frying

1 teaspoon sea salt

½ teaspoon ground pepper

The Spicy Sriracha Aioli, or the
dip of your choice

batter

225 ml/8 fl oz unsweetened
non-dairy milk

1 tablespoon apple cider vinegar

4 tablespoons Tabasco buffalo-
style hot sauce

2 teaspoons cornflour

260 g/9 oz plain flour

1 tablespoon sea salt

1 tablespoon chilli powder

2 teaspoons garlic powder

2 teaspoons onion powder

1 teaspoon ground pepper

1 teaspoon ground sage

1 teaspoon ground coriander

1 teaspoon smoked paprika

1 teaspoon celery salt

½ teaspoon ground nutmeg

½ teaspoon ground cinnamon

½ teaspoon ground cumin

½ teaspoon ground allspice

The extremely popular buffalo cauliflower inspired this jacked-up version that's going to bring back all your regretful carnivorous memories of fried chicken! It doesn't get more comforting than this. (Well it does, 'cause you're only two chapters into the book.) I really like this as meaty two-bite pieces, but you could also go for popcorn style or try chicken fried steak style by slicing your cauliflower the way we do with the Buffalo Cauliflower Sandwich (page 103). Serve it up with peas, mashed potatoes and The Gravy (page 220), and you've got yourself one helluva Southern classic!

Preheat the oven to 220°C/425°F/Gas Mark 7.

To prepare the cauliflower, toss the cauliflower on a baking sheet with the 2 tablespoons vegetable oil, salt and ground pepper. Bake for 30 – 35 minutes until tender. Leave to cool if necessary before handling the florets for battering.

Heat the oil for deep-frying in a large heavy-based pot or deep fryer to a temperature of 160°C – 180°C/325°F – 350°F on a deep-frying thermometer. The amount of oil may vary depending on the size of your frying vessel.

To make the batter, combine the non-dairy milk with the apple cider vinegar and hot sauce in a large bowl. Mix the cornflour with a small amount of the milk mixture to make a paste and add to the bowl. This helps avoid lumps.

In another large bowl, combine the flour with the salt and all the spices.

Do not batter the cauliflower and leave it to stand before it goes in the oil. Only coat the pieces once the oil has reached 160°C/325°F. Batter a floret, then coat in the flour mixture, then submerge in the batter again and coat in the flour mixture once again. Fry a few pieces at a time for 4 – 5 minutes until golden brown and crispy.

Remove with a slotted spoon on to a baking sheet or large plate covered with kitchen paper to absorb excess oil.

Serve with the aioli or a dip of your choice.

To reheat leftover fried cauliflower, place the pieces on a baking sheet and bake in a 220°C/425°F/Gas Mark 7 oven for 10 – 12 minutes.

hot tip I prefer these rings deep-fried, but you can bake them if you make the filling from scratch. If you're using leftover Bacon Mac & Cheese (page 131), you'll definitely need to deep-fry the rings or the filling will get overcooked. If baking the rings, arrange on non-stick baking paper-lined baking sheets. I recommend spraying the breaded rings with a light coating of oil. Bake in a preheated 200°C/400°F/Gas Mark 6 oven for 30 minutes, flipping the rings halfway through the bake time.

mac & cheese onion rings

MAKES 6 – 8
PREP TIME 20 minutes, plus
1 – 2 hours for freezing rings
COOK TIME 50 minutes

prep ahead

Mac & Cheese Sauce (page 131)

ingredients

180 g/6½ oz curved macaroni

Mac & Cheese Sauce

5 or 6 (5.5 cm/2¼ inch) onions

1 – 1.4 litres/1¾ – 2½ pints
vegetable oil, for deep-frying

170 g/6 oz panko-style
breadcrumbs

2 teaspoons dried oregano

2 teaspoons dried basil

2 teaspoons sea salt

1 teaspoon chilli powder

200 g/7 oz plain flour

400 ml/14 fl oz unsweetened
non-dairy milk

2 teaspoons egg replacer
powder or cornflour

Hot sauce or ketchup,
for dipping

You're not dreaming – what you're looking at is for real! I've managed to merge two of my favourite things into one drool-worthy morsel. It's creamy mac and cheese stuffed into onion rings, then deep-fried with a crispy seasoned breadcrumb coating.

In a large pot of salted boiling water, cook the macaroni until al dente. Drain but do not rinse. Combine the cooked macaroni with the sauce in a large bowl just before assembling the onion rings. You can also cook the pasta and make the sauce ahead of time but don't combine them until you're ready to assemble the onion rings.

Line 2 baking sheets with non-stick baking paper. Trim the ends of each whole onion so they're flat end to end. Then cut the onions into slices approximately 2 cm/¾ inch thick. Separate the slices into rings and lay them out on the baking sheets.

Fill each ring generously with the sauced macaroni, leaving no gaps and levelling it out on top. The filling shouldn't be mounding beyond the onion ring. Freeze for 1 – 2 hours or until the sauce has solidified. It doesn't need to be rock-solid frozen, but solid enough that nothing falls out when you lift a ring.

When ready to fry, heat the oil in a large heavy-based pot or deep-fryer to a temperature of 180°C – 182°C/350°F – 360°F on a deep-frying thermometer.

In a bowl, combine the breadcrumbs with the oregano, basil, 1½ teaspoons of the salt and the chilli powder. In another bowl, stir together the flour, non-dairy milk, egg replacer and remaining ½ teaspoon salt to make a smooth batter.

Coat a frozen ring in the batter, allowing the excess to drip off, then straight away coat evenly with the breadcrumb mixture.

Work with a few batches at a time and fry immediately for 3 – 4 minutes for large rings and 2½ – 3 minutes for small rings. Flip the pieces halfway through frying. Remove them with a slotted spoon on to baking sheets lined with kitchen paper. The rings are best served immediately with hot sauce or ketchup for dipping. They're also great leftover and cold, or you can reheat them in an oven or microwave until warmed through.

spicy black bean taquitos

SERVES 4 – 6
PREP TIME 45 minutes
COOK TIME 15 – 20 minutes

prep ahead

The Nacho Cheese (page 205)

The Guac Sauce (page 209)

The Soured Cream (page 210)

ingredients

1 small onion, halved

6 salad onions, white and green parts, roughly chopped

4 garlic cloves

½ teaspoon ground cumin

1 teaspoon chilli powder

250 g/11½ oz cooked black beans, or 539 g/19 oz canned black beans, rinsed and drained

1 jalapeño chilli pepper, seeded and diced (use half a jalapeño for mild)

140 g/5 oz thawed frozen sweetcorn

55 g/2 oz diced red pepper (about ½ pepper)

3 teaspoons vegetable oil, plus 125 ml/4 fl oz for frying

350 ml/12 fl oz The Nacho Cheese

20 (15 cm/6 inch) corn tortillas

The Guac Sauce, to serve

The Soured Cream, to serve

These black bean taquitos are a fun and easy party dish or can even make a great main event if you serve them with toppings like shredded lettuce, chopped tomato or salsa, and a chunkier guacamole. Yes, I'm suggesting you make a taquito salad. You can thank me later!

Process the onion halves, salad onions, garlic, cumin and chilli powder in a food processor until very finely chopped. Add the beans, jalapeño, sweetcorn and pepper, and run the food processor a few times just to get everything very finely chopped, but don't process so much that the mixture becomes a smooth mash.

Heat a large cast-iron frying pan or heavy-based pan over a medium heat with 1 teaspoon of the vegetable oil. Add the mixture from the food processor and cook for 3 – 4 minutes, stirring occasionally, until soft and fragrant.

Pour the mixture into a large bowl. Add the cheese and stir to combine well.

Wipe out the pan and coat it with 1 teaspoon of the vegetable oil heated over a medium-low heat. Place 2 – 3 tortillas in the pan to warm up, flipping once or twice. This step may be unnecessary if you're using flour tortillas or have very fresh corn tortillas. I always find they're a little dry, and this will help with rolling the taquitos. Add the remaining 1 teaspoon vegetable oil to the pan after warming a few tortillas, if necessary. As you remove the warmed tortillas from the pan, start rolling them up. Place about 2 tablespoons of filling on one-third of a tortilla and shape into a log, rolling tightly and tucking one end under. Place the filled tortillas seam side down on baking sheets.

Once all the tortillas are warmed, leave the pan over the heat and add the 125 ml/4 fl oz vegetable oil for frying.

Place the taquitos seam side down in the hot frying oil. They should sizzle immediately or else the oil isn't hot enough. Fry in batches for 3 – 4 minutes, flipping the taquitos halfway through. Lower the heat if necessary. Remove the fried taquitos to kitchen paper to absorb excess oil.

Serve immediately with The Guac Sauce and Soured Cream.

hot tip I very much prefer deep-fried taquitos, but if you must bake them, preheat the oven to 200°C/400°F/Gas Mark 6. There is no need to cook the filling before baking. Place the rolled taquitos seam side down on non-stick baking paper-lined baking sheets. Spray with a light coating of oil and bake for 15 minutes, flipping the taquitos halfway through the bake time, until golden and slightly crisp. They will not get as crispy as the deep-fried version!

crispy crabless cakes

MAKES 10 cakes
PREP TIME 30 minutes
COOK TIME 15 minutes

prep ahead

The Horseradish-dill Aioli
(page 226)

crabless cakes

200 g/7 oz drained marinated
artichoke hearts, finely chopped,
plus 2 tablespoons liquid

35 g/1¼ oz finely chopped
shallot (about 1 small shallot)

65 g/2¼ oz finely chopped
celery (about 1 stick)

1 teaspoon freshly squeezed
lemon juice

60 g/2¼ oz chickpea flour

2 teaspoons coconut sugar
or brown sugar

1 teaspoon Old Bay seasoning

¼ teaspoon sea salt

¼ teaspoon ground pepper

225 – 475 ml/8 – 6 fl oz
vegetable oil, for frying

The Horseradish-dill Aioli

breading

30 g/1 oz chickpea flour

75 g/2¾ oz multigrain
breadcrumbs

125 ml/4 fl oz unsweetened
non-dairy milk

The first time I had a vegan crab cake I was shook! John and I were eating at Lakeside (Wynn Hotel) in Las Vegas and devoured chef Tal Ronnen's crab cakes in seconds. There was no way I could get access to his secret recipe, but I carefully examined every bite so I could figure it out at home. There are a lot of vegan crab cake recipes made from artichokes or hearts of palm floating around the Internet, and while they're all pretty delicious, ours has been tried and tested by many former seafood addicts who claim they'd rather eat this than the real thing any day!

If you're based in the UK, search out Old Bay seasoning online.

To make the crabless cakes, place all the ingredients, except the oil and aioli, in a large bowl. Combine well with a fork. It's important that the artichokes, shallots and celery are very small and uniformly chopped so that the cakes will stick together while frying.

You should have a 1 cm/½ inch of vegetable oil in a large cast-iron frying pan or other heavy-based pan for frying. Heat it to a temperature of 180°C – 182°C/350°F – 360°F on a deep-frying thermometer.

To make the breading, place the chickpea flour in a wide, shallow dish. Use another shallow dish for the breadcrumbs and a bowl for the milk.

Take 4 tablespoons of the crabless cake mixture and press and form it into a thick patty with your hands. Gently place the cake in the chickpea flour and coat all sides evenly. Quickly submerge it in the milk and make sure all the flour looks wet. Remove it from the milk and place in the breadcrumbs. Using your hands, coat all sides of the cake well in the breadcrumbs, then lightly shake off any excess. Set the coated cakes on a plate or baking sheet. Once they're all assembled, immediately deep-fry in batches.

Delicately place 2 or 3 cakes in the hot oil. Fry for about 4 minutes until golden brown, flipping halfway through. Gently remove the cakes with a slotted spoon and place on kitchen paper to absorb any excess oil.

Serve immediately with the aioli. Leftovers can be heated over a medium heat in a pan lightly coated with vegetable oil.

veggie sides & big salads

Not including too many salads or raw vegetables in this cookbook was completely intentional. Comfort food really needs to be warm! But I do love transforming vegetables and elevating their flavour, so here are a few lighter ideas for when you need a break from all the robust recipes. Vegetables are always the stars in vegan cooking, but here they shine bright in all their colourful glory! And they still feel indulgent, not pious, I promise.

lemony parm green beans

SERVES 4 – 6
PREP TIME 15 minutes
COOK TIME 10 minutes

prep ahead

The Parm (page 207)

ingredients

900 g/2 lb green beans

2 teaspoons olive oil

1 shallot, finely sliced

Juice of ½ lemon, plus grated zest from 1 lemon

Sea salt and ground pepper

4 tablespoons The Parm

This is how I grew up eating green beans. For all I know my mom got this recipe from a magazine in the late '80s, but it remains my favourite way to eat my veggies. The lemon brings a fresh brightness to this dish, and if it lights you up, give it a try on broccoli, cauliflower, mangetout or kale too!

Wash the green beans and trim the stems.

Heat a large cast-iron frying pan or heavy-based pan over a medium heat. When it's hot, add the olive oil and green beans. Sauté for 4 – 5 minutes, tossing occasionally.

Add the shallot and continue to cook for 3 – 4 minutes, again only tossing occasionally, allowing the shallots to caramelize.

Add the lemon juice and salt and pepper to taste and cook for another minute or so. The beans should be bright green and not overcooked or too wilted.

Turn off the heat and add the lemon zest and The Parm and toss to coat well.

Serve immediately in the pan or arrange on a serving platter.

mushroom & herb toast

MAKES 4
PREP TIME 25 minutes
COOK TIME 10 minutes

prep ahead

The Parm (page 207)

ingredients

- 225 g/8 oz chanterelle mushrooms
- 225 g/8 oz shiitake mushrooms
- 4 tablespoons olive oil
- ½ teaspoon finely chopped fresh rosemary
- ½ teaspoon fresh thyme leaves
- 2 tablespoons finely chopped fresh flat-leaf parsley
- 4 tablespoons white wine
- ¼ teaspoon sea salt
- ¼ teaspoon ground pepper
- 1 tablespoon freshly squeezed lemon juice
- 4 slices sourdough bread
- 4 tablespoons The Parm

Mushrooms are truly a magical culinary gift. Their earthy flavour and hearty texture make them absolutely one of my favourite ingredients. Here I use shiitakes and chanterelles, and when you try this you'll understand why these fancy varieties attract all the attention like the fun guys they are! They get a quick sauté in fresh herbs and are served mounded on scrumptious sourdough.

Preheat the oven to 230°C/450°F/Gas Mark 8 if toasting the bread in the oven.

Do not wash the mushrooms under running water; rather, take a damp cloth or kitchen paper and brush off any visible dirt or debris. Trim the bottom 5 mm/¼ inch of the chanterelle stems and trim the woody part of the shiitake stems if necessary. Slice the chanterelles and any large shiitakes. If the shiitakes are fairly small, I prefer leaving them whole.

Heat a cast-iron frying pan over a medium heat with 2 tablespoons of the olive oil. Sauté the mushrooms with the rosemary, thyme and parsley for about 4 minutes. Add the white wine, salt and pepper and cook for a further 2 – 3 minutes until most of the liquid is evaporated.

Add the lemon juice and cook for 1 minute.

Meanwhile, brush the sourdough slices with the remaining 2 tablespoons olive oil and either grill oil side down in a grill pan or toast oil side up on a baking sheet in the oven until golden brown.

Top each slice with a mound of mushrooms and garnish with about 1 tablespoon of The Parm. Serve immediately!

green curry cauliflower roast

SERVES 4 – 6
PREP TIME 20 minutes
COOK TIME 55 minutes

ingredients

60 g/2¼ oz finely chopped onion (about ½ onion)

2 garlic cloves, very finely chopped

2 tablespoons vegetable oil

1 can (400 ml/14 fl oz) full-fat coconut milk

3 kaffir lime leaves

2 tablespoons coarsely chopped Thai basil

1 tablespoon maple syrup

2 tablespoons green curry paste

½ teaspoon sea salt

1 tablespoon freshly squeezed lime juice

1 large cauliflower

My love for the cauli will never die! It's the blandest-looking vegetable of the bunch and yet has so much flavour hidden away in its deepest corners. Of course, you could cut it up, baste it and roast it in anything you want, but there's something about the way a whole cauliflower looks when roasted and caramelized. Honestly, it's just sexy! Plus now you don't have a bunch of cutting to do! This version is done green curry-style, and I like it on its own or served in slabs over brown rice.

Preheat the oven to 200°C/400°F/Gas Mark 6.

In a cast-iron frying pan or ovenproof pan over a medium heat, sauté the onion and garlic in the vegetable oil for approximately 3 minutes until just softened, lowering the heat if necessary to prevent the garlic from burning. Stir in the coconut milk, lime leaves, basil, maple syrup, curry paste, salt and lime juice. Bring to a simmer and cook for 4 – 5 minutes until the curry mixture thickens slightly.

Meanwhile, trim all the leaves from the base of the cauliflower. Trim the thick part of the stalk as much as necessary so the cauliflower can sit flat in the pan.

Place the cauliflower bottom side up in the pan and pour half of the curry mixture on to the bottom, allowing it to seep into the cauliflower florets for a minute. Then flip it right side up and pour the remaining curry mixture over top. The excess will pool around the cauliflower. Use a brush to coat all parts of the cauliflower.

Roast for 45 minutes, basting once or twice during the bake time, until tender and a golden caramelized colour forms on the outside of the cauliflower.

Carve into thick slices and serve immediately.

brussels sprouts caesar salad

SERVES 2 as a main or
4 as a starter
PREP TIME 30 minutes
COOK TIME 45 minutes

prep ahead

Almond Bacon (page 10)

The Parm (page 207)

caesar dressing

1 garlic bulb

3 teaspoons olive oil

2 pinches plus 1 teaspoon
sea salt

90 g/3¼ oz raw cashews,
soaked in hot water for 20
minutes

175 ml/6 fl oz water

1 pitted Medjool date

3½ tablespoons nutritional yeast

1 teaspoon grated lemon zest

3 tablespoons freshly squeezed
lemon juice

1 tablespoon apple cider vinegar

1 teaspoon ground pepper

½ teaspoon Dijon mustard

brussels sprouts

2 tablespoons olive oil

1.1 kg/2 lb 7 oz Brussels
sprouts, halved

1 teaspoon sea salt

½ teaspoon ground pepper

2 tablespoons capers

225 g/8 oz Almond Bacon

4 tablespoons The Parm

Lemon wedges, to serve

Team warm salads unite! Roasted veggies make salads feel cozier and make me feel satisfied no matter what the season. In the summer you can grill the vegetables on the barbecue. Here I've modified our original kale Caesar salad recipe into a hearty filling Caesar salad with roasted brussels sprouts as the base.

Preheat the oven to 200°C/400°F/Gas Mark 6.

To prepare the dressing, peel any excess layers of skin from the garlic bulb, leaving some skin intact. Cut the bulb in half crossways to expose the cloves. Coat each half with 1½ teaspoons of the olive oil and sprinkle with a pinch of salt. Place in a small baking tin and bake for 35 minutes until the cloves are browned and very soft to touch.

Remove the roasted cloves from the bulb and place in a high-powered blender.

Drain and rinse the cashews. Add the cashews and the remaining ingredients to the blender and process on high until very smooth.

You can make the dressing ahead and chill it. But since this salad is meant to be served warm, allow the dressing to stand at room temperature before serving to take the chill off. If you make it fresh with the roasted garlic, the dressing will be slightly warm already and can be served on the salad immediately.

To prepare the Brussels sprouts, heat a large cast-iron frying pan over a medium-high heat. Once the pan is hot, add the olive oil, Brussels sprouts, salt and ground pepper. Cook for 10 – 12 minutes, stirring occasionally, to develop some golden brown colour.

In a bowl, toss the warm Brussels sprouts with the capers and 125 ml/ 4 fl oz of the dressing until well combined. Top with the bacon and The Parm and serve with extra dressing and lemon wedges. This salad is nice served with toasted or grilled sourdough topped with vegan butter as well.

banh mi bowl

SERVES 4
PREP TIME 30 minutes
COOK TIME 50 minutes

prep ahead

The Jalapeño-lime Aioli
(page 227)

The BBQ Sauce (page 209)

ingredients

1 (450 g/16 oz) block medium-firm or firm tofu

2 tablespoons cornflour

125 ml/4 fl oz The BBQ Sauce or shop-bought sauce

270 g/9½ oz stemmed and shredded or finely chopped kale

240 g/8½ oz shredded or finely chopped Chinese cabbage

4 tablespoons The Jalapeño-lime Aioli, plus extra for drizzling

3 salad onions, white and green parts, roughly chopped

270 g/9½ oz grated or ribboned carrot (about 1 large carrot)

270 g/9½ oz grated or ribboned cucumber (about 1 cucumber)

40 g/1½ oz roughly chopped coriander

50 g/1½ oz sliced pickled or fresh jalapeño chilli peppers

Here you have a deconstructed Vietnamese sandwich known as a *banh mi*. That doesn't mean that this bowl couldn't very well get dressed up with a baguette to become a sandwich once again. Just slice the tofu instead of cubing it. That's how many of the recipes in this book work once you're familiar with them; you can use them interchangeably and tweak them to your taste. When you get to the Stacked Sandwiches chapter (page 90), you'll see how even many of those components can transition back to salads. The only limit is your imagination.

Preheat the oven to 220°C/425°F/Gas Mark 7.

Drain the excess water from the tofu and pat dry with a tea towel or kitchen paper. Cut into small cubes. Toss the cubes in the cornflour and lay out on a baking sheet, spacing the cubes 5 mm/¼ inch apart. Bake for 30 – 40 minutes until golden and crispy. There isn't really a need to flip the pieces while baking unless you find your oven bakes unevenly.

Toss the crispy tofu in the BBQ sauce in a bowl. Lay out the cubes on the baking sheet, spacing them 5 mm/¼ inch apart once again. Reserve any excess sauce to toss with the tofu just before assembling the bowls. Bake for 10 minutes.

To assemble the bowls, toss the kale and cabbage together in a large bowl with the aioli and the chopped salad onions. Toss to coat well.

Place the dressed greens in serving bowls. Top with the carrot, cucumber, coriander, jalapeños and tofu. Drizzle with more aioli, if you like.

hot tip If you want more pickle, top the bowls with Pickled Red Onions (page 107) and/or submerge the carrot and cucumber in equal parts rice vinegar and warm water, with 1 teaspoon each sugar and salt. Leave to stand for 20 minutes.

my big fat greek potato salad

SERVES 6 – 8
PREP TIME 45 minutes, plus
marinating for 3 hours or overnight
COOK TIME 45 minutes

prep ahead

The Creamy Cucumber
(page 223)

tofu feta

1 (400 g/14 oz) block firm
or extra-firm tofu

125 ml/4 fl oz white wine
vinegar

1 tablespoon freshly squeezed
lemon juice

125 ml/4 fl oz unsweetened soy
or almond milk

1 teaspoon dried basil

2 garlic cloves, very finely
chopped

2 teaspoons sea salt

salad

900 g/2 lb small white or red
potatoes, halved

1 tablespoon olive oil

1 teaspoon dried oregano

½ teaspoon sea salt

½ teaspoon ground pepper

300 g/10½ oz diced cucumber
(about 1 cucumber)

220 g/8 oz diced green pepper
(about 2 peppers)

340 g/12 oz cherry tomatoes,
halved

2 red onions, diced

90 g/3¼ oz pitted Kalamata
olives

6 – 8 padron peppers

The Creamy Cucumber

Dried oregano, to serve

This is a potato salad with substance, and it'll get you stoked for a beach day or picnic with your pals. It's got chunks of all things Greek and is a welcome change from the typical variation. You could even swap rotini or macaroni for the potatoes for a big fat Greek pasta salad.

To prepare the tofu feta, drain the excess water from the tofu and pat and press it dry between kitchen paper or a tea towel. You don't need to get all the water out, just some of it. Cut the tofu into 1 cm/½-inch cubes.

Whisk together the vinegar, lemon juice, non-dairy milk, basil, garlic and salt in a glass container with a fitted lid. Submerge the tofu cubes in the mixture, place the lid on the container and chill. Marinate the tofu overnight for a strong flavour, but you can marinate it for as little as 3 hours.

To prepare the salad, preheat the oven to 200°C/400°F/Gas Mark 6.

Toss the potatoes in the olive oil, oregano, salt and pepper in a baking dish. Bake for 45 minutes, tossing once halfway through the bake time, until roasted and golden brown.

Toss the warm potatoes with the cucumber, pepper, tomatoes, onion, olives, pepperoncini and tofu feta. Drizzle with as much creamy cucumber dressing as you like and serve immediately. Add extra ground pepper and/or oregano to taste.

Be sure to dress only the amount you will consume. If you're not eating the salad straight away, do not toss the potatoes with the veggies, as the cucumber and tomatoes will get soggy.

southwest chop salad

SERVES 4
PREP TIME 25 minutes

prep ahead

The Classic Ranch (page 223)

Coconut Bacon (page 9)

ingredients

600 g/1 lb 5 oz finely chopped Cos lettuce (1 large head)

115 g/4 oz finely chopped red onion (about 1 onion)

200 g/10 oz fresh or frozen and thawed sweetcorn kernels

320 g/11¼ oz cooked black beans, or 539 g/19 oz canned black beans, rinsed and drained

340 g/12 oz cherry tomatoes, halved

1 large avocado, stoned, peeled and diced

225 g/8 oz Coconut Bacon

The Classic Ranch

This is a fast and fresh salad that I rely on often. Usually I prep all the components ahead of time and store everything separately so I'm ready for quick assembly throughout the week. That's about as organized as I get when it comes to nourishing myself, so this is what I turn to when I need to reset. And if you didn't notice, this salad also gifts you with the makings of a pretty nice veggie taco too!

Assemble each salad with 150 g/5½ oz of the chopped Cos, 30 g/1 oz of the diced onion and 70 g/2 oz each of the corn, beans and tomatoes, plus one quarter of the avocado.

Top with the bacon and ranch dressing. Feel free to go wild on those two things too!

hot tip Wanna make this salad warm? Sauté the black beans, sweetcorn and red onion together with the spices of your choice, and leave the rest of the ingredients raw and fresh. Ummm, also taco worthy!

hearty soups

This chapter is like taking a leisurely stroll down the canned soup aisle at the supermarket and throwing everything into your trolley. Maybe one day we'll live in a world where vegans could actually do that without worrying about the ingredient list, but even if we could, nothing compares to homemade. To make soups efficiently, chop and prep all your ingredients in advance so you're just throwing stuff into the pot at the right time and not overcooking or undercooking ingredients. These hearty soups are comforting, clean and cosy so slurp 'em up with pride and use them as inspo to concoct your own from-scratch soups whenever the urge strikes!

hot tip This recipe will probably leave you with unused puff pastry. The benefit of not using real butter or animal lard is you can you can refreeze it! Roll it out to 3 mm/⅛ inch thick and place between clingfilm. Fold it over itself and place in the freezer for another use. Thaw before using once again.

chicken potpie soup

SERVES 6
PREP TIME 1 hour
COOK TIME 35 minutes

ingredients

280 g/10 oz peeled and diced white or yellow potatoes (about 2 potatoes)

2 tablespoons arrowroot flour or plain flour

475 ml/16 fl oz unsweetened soya milk

2 tablespoons vegetable oil

250 g/8⅘ oz finely chopped vegan chicken-style fillets (such as Quorn)

115 g/4 oz finely chopped onion (about 1 onion)

120 g/4¼ oz finely chopped carrot (about 1 large carrot)

135 g/4¾ oz finely chopped celery (about 2 sticks)

3 garlic cloves, very finely chopped

1 teaspoon mustard powder

1 teaspoon fresh thyme

½ teaspoon ground basil

½ teaspoon ground sage

½ teaspoon sea salt

½ teaspoon ground pepper

1 vegan chicken-flavoured bouillon cube dissolved in 475 ml/16 fl oz water, or 475 ml/16 fl oz low-salt vegetable stock

140 g/5 oz fresh or frozen sweetcorn

115 g/4 oz fresh or frozen peas

10 g/¼ oz fresh flat-leaf parsley, finely chopped

1 (500 g/1 lb 2 oz) packet frozen vegan puff pastry, thawed in the fridge

35 g/1¼ oz plain flour, for rolling out pastry

I don't want to argue about whether this is a chicken potpie or a chicken potpie soup. It's both! But the chicken potpies I recall eating when the babysitter was over – which were from a box BTW – had the thickest, gooiest filling that I didn't find that appetizing. So I thinned it out to my liking and called it soup! It's my book, and I can do what I want. Regardless, it's spot-on and delish. You can ditch the puff pastry topping and pair the soup with Flaky Buttermilk Scones (page 15) or a crusty loaf of bread for dipping.

Bring a pot of cold water and the potatoes to the boil and cook for 8 – 10 minutes until tender. Drain and add 140 g/5 oz of the potatoes to a high-powered blender with the arrowroot flour and soya milk. Blend until smooth and set aside.

Preheat the oven to 220°C/425°F/Gas Mark 7.

Heat a large stockpot over a medium heat with the vegetable oil and sauté the vegan chicken-style fillets for about 4 minutes until lightly browned. Add the onion, carrot, celery, garlic, mustard, thyme, basil, sage, salt and pepper. Sauté for 5 minutes, stirring occasionally, until the veggies are softened and half cooked.

Add a bit of stock to lift the brown bits off the bottom of the pot. Slowly add the blended potato mixture, bring to a low simmer and stir constantly while it thickens slightly. Add the remaining stock, remaining potatoes, sweetcorn, peas and parsley. Bring to a simmer and cook for 5 minutes. Turn off the heat and cover the pot while you prepare the puff pastry.

Some pre-made puff pastry is already rolled out thin and ready to use; others may need to be rolled out. Either way, place the pastry on a lightly floured surface. Roll out with a floured rolling pin to 3 mm/⅛ inch thick. Stop to check under the pastry and lightly flour again so it doesn't stick. Use ovenproof bowls or ramekins for the soup. Trace rounds on the pastry 5 mm/¼ inch larger than the bowls and cut out the rounds.

Ladle the soup into the bowls and place the bowls on a baking sheet. Brush the edges of each bowl with a bit of soup and place a pastry round on top, gently pressing the edges to seal.

Bake for 10 – 12 minutes until the pastry is golden brown and puffed. Serve immediately!

real wonton soup

SERVES 4;
35 – 40 wontons
PREP TIME 50 minutes
COOK TIME 10 minutes

wontons

115 g/4 oz shiitake mushrooms, stemmed

½ large carrot, peeled

2 garlic cloves

1 salad onion, white and green parts

90 g/3¼ oz crumbled medium-firm tofu

1 teaspoon sea salt

¼ teaspoon smoked paprika

2 teaspoons toasted sesame oil

2 teaspoons seasoned rice vinegar

35 – 40 vegan wonton wrappers

broth

1 tablespoon toasted sesame oil, plus extra to serve if you like

6 salad onions, white and green parts, finely chopped and kept separate

1 tablespoon very finely chopped or grated ginger

2 garlic cloves, very finely chopped

240 g/8½ oz shredded or finely chopped Chinese cabbage

1 tablespoon seasoned rice vinegar

1 tablespoon vegetarian oyster sauce or low-salt tamari or soy sauce

1 litre/1¾ pints low-salt vegetable stock

475 ml/16 fl oz water

1 teaspoon sea salt

This wonton soup is one of my favourite things in the book. It's highly satisfying and flavourful and tastes spot-on to restaurant-style wonton soup, with a simple gingery broth and dumplings filled with shiitake mushrooms and tofu. I have a special place for it in my comfort food memory bank because it essentially fuelled me during the final months of the writing process! What's also magnificent is that the broth and wontons are easy to freeze so you can have this soup at the ready whenever you need to warm up your tummy.

To make the wontons, it's best to use a food processor for the filling, as the ingredients need to be very finely chopped. Very finely chop the mushrooms, carrot, garlic and salad onion in the food processor. Add to a bowl.

Add the tofu, salt, paprika, sesame oil and vinegar to the finely chopped vegetables. Stir to combine well. The filling can be made in advance and left in the fridge overnight if you want to prep ahead.

Get a small bowl of water for sealing the wontons. Place about 2 scant teaspoons filling in the centre of a wonton wrapper. Wet half of the edge of the wrapper and fold into a half-moon shape, pressing the wrapper and trying to remove any excess air around the edges and in the filling. If using square wrappers, fold into a triangle. Pinch the corners, lift the wonton slightly and use an index finger to gently press into the bottom centre as you slightly overlap and pinch together the two corners. Use an extra dab of water if needed to help the corners stick together. The final result will look like a tortellini. Lay each finished wonton on a lightly floured baking sheet and cover with a tea towel as you assemble them all. Leave covered while you make the broth.

Bring a pot of water to a rolling boil for cooking the wontons.

To make the broth, add the sesame oil to a stockpot over a medium heat and sauté the white parts of the salad onion, ginger and garlic for 2 minutes until just softened and fragrant. Add the cabbage and continue to sauté for 2 minutes. Lower the heat if necessary to prevent the garlic from burning.

CONTINUED

Stir in the vinegar and oyster sauce and cook for 1 minute. Add the vegetable stock, water and salt. Cover, bring to a simmer and cook for 5 minutes.

Meanwhile, add the wontons to the pot of boiling water. They will take about 2 minutes to cook. Once they float to the surface, they're done. Remove them with a slotted spoon to serving bowls (9 or 10 wontons per serving).

Add the broth to each serving bowl. Top with the green parts of the salad onions and extra sesame oil, if you like.

You can freeze the uncooked wontons between layers of non-stick baking paper in a container or freezer bag for up to 2 months. Boil the frozen wontons, without thawing, per the instructions.

hot tip Medium-firm tofu is the best texture for the filling, but if you can't find it, you can use firm. If your crumbled tofu seems quite wet, drain it by squeezing out excess water through a fine-mesh nylon sieve, nut milk bag or double layer of muslin.

gooey french onion soup

SERVES 4 – 6
PREP TIME 25 minutes
COOK TIME 75 minutes

prep ahead

The Mozza (page 208)

onion soup

960 g/2 lb 2 oz thinly sliced onions (about 6 onions)

4 tablespoons vegan butter

2 bay leaves

1 tablespoon fresh thyme leaves

1 – 2 teaspoons sea salt

½ teaspoon ground pepper

2 garlic cloves, very finely chopped

1 tablespoon plain flour

2 tablespoons vegan Worcestershire sauce

175 ml/6 fl oz dry white wine or low-salt vegetable stock

2 vegan beef-flavoured bouillon cubes dissolved in 1.4 litres/ 2½ pints hot water, or 1.4 litres/2½ pints low-salt vegetable stock

croutons

4 – 6 thick slices of baguette

The Mozza

Fresh thyme leaves, to garnish

This soup is such a classic comfort and one of the easiest to make. Getting the flavours balanced just right for a simple but rich onion broth is easy. . . it's cutting all the onions that'll have you in tears! But the water works are so worth it once you slurp up your first hot spoonful and bite into the sopped up crouton with gooey vegan mozza on top.

To make the soup, in a large stockpot over a medium heat, sauté the onions with the butter for 3 – 4 minutes until soft and fragrant. Add the bay leaves, thyme, salt and pepper and continue to cook for 12 – 15 minutes, stirring occasionally. If you're using vegan beef-flavoured bouillon instead of vegetable stock, reduce the amount of salt you add here and, if necessary, adjust to taste afterwards.

Once the onions are caramelized to a pale brown, reduce the heat to medium-low, add the garlic and continue to cook, stirring occasionally, for 15 minutes.

Stir in the flour and Worcestershire sauce, stir to coat the onions well and cook for 2 minutes, stirring constantly.

Add the white wine, increase the heat to get it simmering and cook for 2 minutes. You can use stock in place of the wine, but the wine makes the soup especially delicious!

Add the stock and bring to the boil, then lower the heat and simmer for 30 minutes.

While the soup is simmering, make the croutons.

Preheat the oven to 180°C/350°F/Gas Mark 4.

The baguette slices should be a size that will fit submerged in your soup bowls. Place the slices on a baking sheet and toast in the oven for 15 – 18 minutes, flipping them halfway through the bake time. The toast should be quite hard and crusty. Set the croutons aside.

CONTINUED

Set the oven to grill. Place ovenproof bowls on the baking sheet and ladle out the soup. Place a crouton on top slightly submerged in the soup but still floating and visible. Generously spoon some of The Mozza on top of the crouton. Some can go onto the soup out to the edges of each bowl. Set the baking sheet under the grill and grill for 3 – 5 minutes until The Mozza is golden brown and slightly bubbling. Watch closely so it doesn't burn!

Garnish with thyme and serve immediately.

hot tip You can freeze leftovers of the soups in this chapter! Make sure you let the soup cool completely before storing in jars or containers. Thaw the soup in the fridge completely and then heat up to serve!

see food chowder

SERVES 6
PREP TIME 45 minutes
COOK TIME 55 minutes

prep ahead

Tofu Bacon Crumbles (page 10)

ingredients

225 g/8 oz shiitake mushrooms

225 g/8 oz oyster mushrooms

3 tablespoons olive oil

1 teaspoon Old Bay seasoning

½ – 1 teaspoon sea salt

½ teaspoon ground pepper

700 g/1 lb 9 oz small red potatoes, quartered

1 teaspoon fresh thyme leaves

120 g/4½ oz raw cashews, soaked in hot water for 20 minutes

450 ml/16 fl oz water

1 finely chopped onion

1 large finely chopped carrot

2 finely chopped celery sticks

3 garlic cloves, very finely chopped

¼ teaspoon ground cayenne

40 g/1½ oz arrowroot flour or plain flour

1 vegan chicken-flavoured bouillon cube dissolved in 475 ml/16 fl oz hot water, or 475 ml/16 fl oz low-salt vegetable stock

175 ml/6 fl oz dry white wine

225 ml/8 fl oz unsweetened soya milk

4 hearts of palm, thinly sliced

150 g/5 oz frozen sweetcorn kernels

2 tablespoons finely chopped fresh dill

Remember my story about the Crispy Crabless Cakes (page 53) and how John and I ate the most delicious ones at Lakeside (Wynn Hotel) in Las Vegas? Well the inspo for this See Food Chowder is essentially the same. This restaurant was a full seafood restaurant that had an equally great vegan menu with plant-based versions of things you didn't think you could ever find! And when I see food, more importantly anything that says the word vegan before it, I eat it! Then I re-create it, and now you lucky clams don't even need to go there 'cause you get this tasty rendition right here.

If you're based in the UK, search out Old Bay seasoning online.

Preheat the oven to 220°C/425°F/Gas Mark 7.

Leave most of the mushrooms whole, trim any woody stems from the shiitakes and roughly chop any particularly large shiitake or oyster mushrooms.

Toss the mushrooms on a baking sheet with 1 tablespoon of the olive oil, the Old Bay seasoning and ¼ teaspoon each of the salt and pepper.

On another baking sheet, toss the potatoes with 1 tablespoon of the olive oil, the thyme and the remaining ¼ teaspoon each of salt and pepper.

Bake the mushrooms and potatoes at the same time. Place the mushrooms on the top rack; they'll take 13 – 15 minutes, depending on the size, until roasted and crispy in some spots. Place the potatoes on the middle rack; they'll take about 20 minutes until roasted and slightly crispy on the outside.

Meanwhile, drain and rinse the cashews and blend together with the water in a high-powered blender until very smooth.

In a large stockpot over a medium heat, sauté the onion, carrot and celery in the remaining 1 tablespoon olive oil for 4 – 5 minutes until softened and half cooked. Add the garlic and cayenne and sauté for 2 minutes. Lower the heat slightly to prevent burning.

Add the flour and stir constantly for 2 minutes. Once it's a little sticky

CONTINUED

2 tablespoons finely chopped
fresh flat-leaf parsley

2 tablespoons finely chopped
nori seaweed

Tofu Bacon Crumbles,
to garnish

Fresh dill sprigs or finely
chopped fresh flat-leaf parsley,
to garnish

Oyster crackers or vegan buttery
crackers, to serve (optional)

and quite dry in the pot, add a bit of the stock to loosen and smooth out
the mixture.

Continue stirring while you add the wine. Bring to a simmer and cook for
2 minutes.

Constantly stir while slowly adding the soya milk and the cashew
mixture and bring to a low simmer. Add the remaining stock and bring
to a low simmer again. Add the mushrooms, potatoes, hearts of palm,
corn, dill, parsley and nori. Heat through for 10 – 15 minutes and serve
immediately. Add salt to taste if you used low-salt vegetable stock
instead of bouillon.

Top with the bacon crumbles and garnish with the dill. Serve with oyster
crackers or vegan buttery crackers, if you like.

cream of broccoli soup

SERVES 6
PREP TIME 40 minutes
COOK TIME 30 minutes

ingredients

1 finely chopped onion

1 finely chopped small shallot

4 garlic cloves, very finely chopped

4 tablespoons vegan butter

½ teaspoon celery salt

½ teaspoon ground pepper, plus extra for seasoning

¼ teaspoon smoked paprika

40 g/1½ oz arrowroot flour or plain flour

750 ml/1¼ pints unsweetened non-dairy milk

420 g/1.5 oz finely chopped broccoli florets (about 3 crowns)

2 tablespoons chopped fresh dill

2 tablespoons chopped fresh flat-leaf parsley

750 ml/1¼ pints low-salt vegetable stock

Sea salt

180 g/6½ oz grated vegan Cheddar, to garnish (optional)

Smooth soup vs chunky soup. Which reigns supreme? Well let's not debate each other too much because I'm on team chunk! There's nothing appealing about eating thick puréed soups that resemble baby food. I like chewing, so I keep my soups full of stuff to sink your teeth into! As such, I've made my cream of broccoli soup creamy and silky, but with broccoli florets dancing around the bowl so you still know what you're eating. I know I've pleased some of you with this decision, and as for the rest of you, you can blend the whole thing into sludge. I'll still love you!

In a large stockpot over a medium heat, sauté the onion, shallot and garlic in the vegan butter for 2 minutes.

Add the celery salt, pepper and smoked paprika and sauté for a further 2 minutes, lowering the heat slightly to prevent the garlic from burning.

Add the flour and stir constantly for 1 minute.

Slowly add 475 ml/16 fl oz of the non-dairy milk while stirring constantly and bring to a simmer. Once the mixture is bubbling and thickened, add the broccoli and continue to stir constantly for 3 minutes. Once there is a smooth roux surrounding the broccoli florets, add the remaining 225 ml/8 fl oz of non-dairy milk and continue to stir for 2 minutes. The broccoli should be slightly tender but still bright green. Add the dill and parsley and continue to cook for another minute. Add 225 ml/8 fl oz of the stock and stir to combine.

Use a slotted spoon to remove about 90 g/3¼ oz of the broccoli and other veg, straining the excess liquid as best you can, and reserve the veg in a bowl. Or if you're a baby, skip this step.

Blend the remaining soup in a blender until smooth or use an immersion blender in the pot. Add the soup back to the pot if you put it in a blender. Add the reserved broccoli and other veg along with the remaining 475 ml/16 fl oz stock. Season with salt and ground pepper to taste. Bring to a low simmer and heat through for 10 minutes. The soup should still be fairly bright green as opposed to brown-green. Serve with grated Cheddar on top, if you like.

curried butternut squash soup

SERVES 6
PREP TIME 50 minutes
COOK TIME 50 minutes

ingredients

1 (900 g/2 lb) butternut squash, peeled and cubed

2 tablespoons olive oil

1¼ teaspoons sea salt

¾ teaspoon ground pepper

1 finely chopped onion (about 115 g/4 oz)

1 large finely chopped carrot (about 120 g/4¼ oz)

2 finely chopped celery stalks (about 135 g/4¾ oz)

4 garlic cloves, very finely chopped

1 bay leaf

2 teaspoons fresh thyme leaves

1 teaspoon dried basil

1 teaspoon yellow curry powder

½ teaspoon ground fenugreek

½ teaspoon paprika

140 g/5 oz frozen sweetcorn kernels

2 diced vine tomatoes (about 170 g/6 oz)

1.4 litres/2½ pints low-salt vegetable stock

225 g/9 oz green beans, cut into 2.5 cm/1 inch pieces

1 400 ml (13.5 fl oz) tin full-fat coconut milk

20 g/¾ oz roughly chopped fresh coriander

1 tablespoon finely chopped fresh mint

180 g/6½ oz baby spinach leaves

A spiced and satiating coconut curry broth mixed with fresh herbs and lots of veggies is my kind of soup for cold days or head colds! The butternut squash is obviously the fearless leader in this soup so I wanted to roast it before stirring it into the soup to give it an extra depth of flavour. Repurpose leftovers of this soup into a thicker curry served over rice or with rice noodles. Just add more full-fat coconut milk and maybe a little extra curry powder or paste to taste. Heat through and simmer until thick.

Preheat the oven to 220°C/425°F/Gas Mark 7.

Toss the cubed butternut squash on a baking sheet with 1 tablespoon of the olive oil and ¼ teaspoon each of the salt and pepper. Roast for 20 – 25 minutes until tender and golden brown. Set aside.

When the butternut squash has about 10 minutes remaining, begin making the soup in a stockpot. Over a medium heat, sauté the onion, carrot and celery in the remaining 1 tablespoon of olive oil for 4 minutes until just softened.

Add the garlic, bay leaf, thyme, basil, curry powder, fenugreek, paprika, remaining 1 teaspoon salt and remaining ½ teaspoon pepper. Stir together and cook for 3 minutes until the garlic is cooked and fragrant. Lower the heat to prevent the garlic from burning.

Add the sweetcorn and tomatoes and cook for another 4 minutes, stirring occasionally.

Add the stock and bring to a low boil. Once the stock is bubbling, add the green beans and simmer for 5 minutes.

Stir in the coconut milk and bring to a low simmer. Once the liquid is bubbling, add the coriander, mint and butternut squash. Simmer for 5 minutes. Add the spinach and continue cooking for 5 – 10 minutes. Serve immediately!

hot tip I've used canned tomatoes to make this quick, but if you have a preference for homemade, try the fresh flavour of The Red Sauce (page 216). You could also add in vegan beef-style mince (such as Quorn) after sautéeing the courgette and mushrooms for an even meatier version!

comforting lasagne soup

SERVES 6 – 8
PREP TIME 30 minutes
COOK TIME 30 minutes

ingredients

1 finely chopped onion (about 115 g/4 oz)

2 tablespoons olive oil

3 garlic cloves, very finely chopped

1 bay leaf

1 teaspoon dried oregano

¼ teaspoon chilli flakes

1 teaspoon sea salt

1 teaspoon ground pepper

1 large diced courgette (about 360 g/12 oz)

240 g/8½ oz sliced chestnut mushrooms

4 tablespoons tomato purée

2 tablespoons balsamic vinegar

2 teaspoons brown sugar

15 g/½ oz finely chopped fresh basil

15 g/½ oz fresh flat-leaf parsley, finely chopped

2 cans (around 794 g/28 oz) chopped tomatoes

2 vegan beef-flavoured bouillon cubes dissolved in 1.8 litres/3¼ pints hot water, or 1.4 litres/2½ pints low-salt vegetable stock and 475 ml/16 fl oz water

12 lasagne sheets (not quick cooking)

300 g/10½ oz baby spinach leaves

Vegan ricotta cheese or grated vegan mozzarella, to garnish (optional)

Why lasagne soup you might be wondering? Well, sure, it's Pinterest worthy, but it's also a new way to savour more lasagne goodness! And lasagne might be the king of comfort food. Regular hot for foodies might know the best vegan lasagne recipe on the blog, so if you think I've gone too far with this, go ahead and stick to the straight and narrow. But if you love love love lasagne like I do, I promise you'll be obsessed with it as a soup.

In a large stockpot over a medium heat, sauté the onion in the olive oil for 2 minutes until just softened.

Add the garlic, bay leaf, oregano, chilli flakes, salt and pepper and continue to sauté for 1 – 2 minutes, stirring constantly. Lower the heat to prevent the garlic from burning.

Add the courgette and mushrooms and cook, stirring occasionally, for 6 minutes until most of the water from the vegetables is released and evaporates.

Add the tomato purée, vinegar, sugar, basil and parsley and stir to combine. Cook for 2 minutes.

Add the tomatoes and stock. Break up the lasagne into smaller pieces and add to the pot. Bring to the boil and simmer for 10 – 12 minutes until the pasta is al dente. Stir occasionally to prevent the pasta from sticking and add the spinach in the last 2 minutes of cooking.

Serve immediately and garnish individual servings with dollops of vegan ricotta or top with grated vegan mozzarella, if you like.

The pasta will absorb liquid if you have leftovers, so reheat the soup with extra water or stock to loosen the pasta, or enjoy the soup when it's thick like a stew.

stacked sandwiches

When I'm unsure of what I want to eat, which happens a lot, I always remember that my foodie soul will be become enlightened by a sandwich. Why? Because. . . bread. Bread gives me life. This chapter celebrates all the wonderful things you can stack between buns and bread. We're going to travel the world together with this sandwich selection, from New Orleans to Philly, Greece to Japan, England to Monte Cristo. Wait, that last one isn't a place?! But you'll definitely want to try the sandwich. To infinity and beyond!

oyster mushroom po' boy

MAKES 4 sandwiches
PREP TIME 45 minutes
COOK TIME 15 minutes

prep ahead

The Thousand Island (page 223)

fried oyster mushrooms

2 tablespoons ground flaxseed

6 tablespoons water

225 ml/8 fl oz unsweetened non-dairy milk

4 tablespoons apple cider vinegar

2 tablespoons vegan oyster sauce or vegan Worcestershire sauce

2 teaspoons garlic powder

2 teaspoons dried basil

1 teaspoon ground white or black pepper

225 g/8 oz oyster mushrooms (16 – 20)

1 – 1.4 litres/1¾ – 2½ pints vegetable oil, for frying

breading

20 g/¾ oz panko-style breadcrumbs

25 g/1 oz polenta

35 g/1¼ oz plain flour

1 teaspoon sea salt

1 teaspoon ground cayenne

1 teaspoon garlic powder

1 teaspoon dried basil

½ teaspoon smoked paprika

½ teaspoon ground pepper

sandwiches

4 hot dog-style buns

The Thousand Island

190 g/7 oz finely chopped Cos lettuce

3 vine tomatoes, thinly sliced

3 gherkins, sliced into rounds

This is my tribute to Guy Fieri, the host of *Diners, Drive-Ins, and Dives!* I equally loathe and am enamoured with his show on the Food Network, as well as with Guy himself. On one hand I want nothing to do with him and what his food stands for, yet on the other hand I want to BE him. I just would never be caught dead in a flame shirt! So I wanted to make a version of a po' boy sandwich because there's always one of these on Triple D. Prawns, lobster, crab, oysters, you name it, Guy finds it, and they're all over America, not just in New Orleans (where the sandwich originated). So sink your big mouth into this sammich and tell me being vegan ain't the greatest! Welcome to flavour town.

To prepare the mushrooms, mix together the ground flaxseed and water in a bowl and leave to stand for 10 minutes to thicken.

In another bowl, mix together the non-dairy milk, vinegar, oyster sauce, garlic powder, basil and pepper. Add the flax mixture and pour the marinade over the mushrooms in a large ziplock bag, making sure they are well submerged. Chill for at least 20 minutes. Or you can leave it overnight.

Heat the oil in a heavy-based pot to a temperature of 185°C – 190°C/365°F – 375°F on a deep-frying thermometer. The oil should be heated to the right temperature just as you're about to bread the mushrooms.

To make the breading, mix together all the ingredients in a bowl.

Remove a few mushrooms from the marinade and place directly in the breading, coating evenly on all sides using your hands. Place each piece in the hot oil and fry for 2 – 3 minutes.

Place fried mushrooms on kitchen paper to absorb excess oil. Continue to bread the mushrooms and fry in small batches.

To assemble the sandwiches, cut the buns in half and toast, if you like. Spread some Thousand Island on the inside of each roll. Layer the Cos lettuce, tomato slices, gherkins and fried mushrooms on one half of each roll. Add more of Thousand Island, if you like. Serve immediately while the oyster mushrooms are still warm.

Reheat leftover fried mushrooms in a 220°C/425°F/Gas Mark 7 oven for 10 – 12 minutes until crispy.

hot tip Try this seitan as a corned beef–style sandwich with spicy mustard and sauerkraut on rye bread!

saved by seitan

MAKES 1 large loaf (enough for both sandwich recipes)
PREP TIME 40 minutes, plus curing seitan overnight
COOK TIME 90 minutes

ingredients

430 g/15 oz vital wheat gluten flour

12 g/½ oz nutritional yeast

2 teaspoons onion powder

1 teaspoon sea salt

1 teaspoon celery salt

1 teaspoon smoked paprika

1 teaspoon garlic powder

1 teaspoon dried thyme

1 teaspoon dried oregano

1 teaspoon dried basil

1 teaspoon ground mustard

1 teaspoon ground pepper

2 vegan beef-flavoured bouillon cubes dissolved in 750 ml/1¼ pints hot water, or 750 ml/1¼ pints low-salt vegetable stock

4 tablespoons vegetable oil

2 tablespoons low-salt tamari or soy sauce

2 tablespoons apple cider vinegar

1 tablespoon tomato purée

I've been saved by seitan! Or maybe I just saved myself because this is the perfect seitan 'beef' for the Philly Cheesesteak (page 96) and Gyro Wrap (page 99). But by all means, get dirty with it and experiment. There are so many ways to make seitan or 'wheat meat' with slightly different textures that work for whatever you're dreaming of making. I achieved a firm, chewy texture here that works when sliced very thin to mimic shaved beef or lamb. So if you're a vegan who craves the carnivorous meals you used to eat, I don't judge or blame you, and I've gotcha covered!

Preheat the oven to 180°C/350°F/Gas Mark 4.

In a large bowl, combine the wheat gluten with the nutritional yeast, spices and herbs.

In another bowl, mix together the stock, vegetable oil, tamari, vinegar and tomato purée until well combined.

Pour the stock mixture into the wheat gluten mixture and stir to combine.

The mixture should be very moist, but still able to be handled as one large piece. It should not be sticking to your hands, but should be quite slippery. You will feel the elasticity of the gluten binding it together into a blob. Place the dough on a clean work surface and knead, pulling and stretching it and folding it over itself a few times. Finally, press it together to form large log shape approximately 25 cm/10 inches long and 12 cm/5 inches in diameter.

Wrap the log tightly in a large piece of heavy-duty foil. You may need to use 2 sheets to make it completely secure. There should be no exposed gaps. Tighten and twist the ends of the foil.

Place the log on a baking sheet and bake for 90 minutes. It should feel very firm when you take it out of the oven. Allow the log to cool at room temperature. Store in the fridge overnight before using it for sandwiches.

The seitan is best sliced very thin with a sharp knife or shaved using a mandolin.

Store the seitan in the fridge and consume within 10 days. Or it can be portioned and wrapped to freeze for longer storage, up to 2 months. Thaw completely before slicing and using in sandwiches.

philly cheesesteak

MAKES 6 sandwiches
PREP TIME 25 minutes
COOK TIME 20 minutes

prep ahead

Saved by Seitan (page 95)

The Nacho Cheese (page 205)

ingredients

2 thinly sliced onions (about 320 g/1¼ oz)

2 thinly sliced green peppers (about 150 g/5½ oz)

2 tablespoons vegetable oil

½ Saved by Seitan loaf, thinly sliced or shaved

2 tablespoons vegan Worcestershire sauce

2 tablespoons water

Sea salt and ground pepper

6 hot dog-style buns

6 tablespoons vegan butter

The Nacho Cheese, warmed

In west Philadelphia, born and raised, on the playground was where I spent most of my days. . . nope not true. But you knew that. Am I the only one whose reference for Philly cheesesteaks comes from watching the *Fresh Prince* drool and reminisce over them in that greasy paper bag? You can find this montage on YouTube, FYI. It always made my mouth water, but I've never eaten one with real steak. Though, I have had my fair share of vegan Philly cheesesteaks and I've really gotta give it up for my own creation. I'm sure you'll agree after just one big bite!

In a large cast-iron frying pan over a medium heat, sauté the onions and peppers with the vegetable oil for 10 – 12 minutes until soft and cooked through. Add the sliced seitan and brown for 3 – 4 minutes.

Combine the Worcestershire sauce and water together in a small bowl. Pour over the vegetables and seitan and toss to coat everything in the sauce. Continue cooking for 3 minutes. Add salt and pepper to taste.

Meanwhile, cut the hot dog buns in half. Toast and butter the buns. Spread the warm cheese on the inside of both halves of each bun. Top with a generous portion of the seitan mixture. Drizzle with more cheese and serve immediately.

gyro wrap

MAKES 6 wraps
PREP TIME 35 minutes
COOK TIME 6 minutes

prep ahead

Saved by Seitan (page 95)

The Creamy Cucumber
(page 223)

ingredients

2 teaspoons vegetable oil

½ Saved by Seitan loaf, thinly
sliced or shaved

½ teaspoon dried oregano

Sea salt and ground pepper

6 large pitta breads

The Creamy Cucumber

300 g/11½ oz baby spinach
or lettuce of your choice

225 g/8 oz alfalfa sprouts
(optional)

2 vine tomatoes, sliced

1 thinly sliced red onion (about
130 g/4½ oz)

150 g/5½ oz thinly sliced
cucumber (about 1 cucumber)

**Make Saved by Seitan (page 95) and you're in sandwich heaven
for a few days. There's enough wheat meat to make both the Philly
Cheesesteak (page 96) and this Greek-inspired gyro wrap! I have to
say, gyro or shawarma meat has to be one of the most unappetizing-
looking things you could eat as an omnivore. I wouldn't touch that stuff
with a 10 foot skewer! Get it? But this super-stuffed wrap has all the
elements you're looking for, is far healthier and The Creamy Cucumber
(page 223) really ties it all together. You can even add the tofu feta
from My Big Fat Greek Potato Salad (page 67) for an extra kick.**

Heat the vegetable oil in a large cast-iron frying pan over a medium heat.
Add the seitan and oregano and season with salt and ground pepper.
Toss together and brown for 5 – 6 minutes.

Meanwhile, warm the pittas in the oven or a toaster, if you like.

Spread some creamy cucumber dressing on each pitta. Place the
spinach, sprouts, tomato slices, onion slices, cucumber slices and a
generous portion of seitan on top. Drizzle more creamy cucumber on top
and roll tightly. Wrap one end of the roll in foil or non-stick baking paper
to contain the contents and serve immediately! You could also stuff
everything inside the pitta and make pockets, but I find they break all
the time.

filet-o-tempeh sandwich

MAKES 4 sandwiches
PREP TIME 35 minutes,
plus 30 minutes to 6 hours
for marinating
COOK TIME 8 minutes

prep ahead

The Tartar Sauce (page 207)

beer-battered tempeh

1 block (225 g/8 oz) tempeh

90 ml/3 fl oz water

90 ml/3 fl oz white wine vinegar

2 tablespoons freshly squeezed
lemon juice

3 teaspoons Old Bay seasoning

2 teaspoons sea salt

1½ teaspoons ground pepper

1 – 1.4 litres/1¼ – 2½ pints
vegetable oil, for frying

130 g/4½ oz plain flour

2 tablespoons baking powder

½ teaspoon paprika

225 ml/8 fl oz cold vegan-
friendly lager or ale

sandwiches

4 wholemeal, sprouted
or sesame seed buns

The Tartar Sauce

150 g/5½ oz sunflower sprouts
or shredded iceberg lettuce

1 avocado, stoned, peeled,
quartered and sliced

Think of this as your ocean-friendly filet-o-fish sandwich. Because we all know the only sustainable seafood is no seafood at all. If you've ever become enamoured with a Planet Earth documentary, you sure as hell have realized how brilliant fish are. I don't want to eat something smarter than me. Anyway, back to the food at hand. Tempeh is one of my favourite plant proteins, but I know a lot of people cringe at it. Me thinks, they had undercooked and underseasoned versions. This tempeh 'fish' was a John creation back in the day, and we thought it needed to become an epic sandwich. So this may be your intro into the world of tempeh, but it's a good one. If you want to swap soda water for the beer, go ahead, but you need the fizz to make the batter nice and fluffy. I love to serve this sandwich with salt and vinegar chips and an icy cold beer!

If you're based in the UK, search out Old Bay seasoning online.

To marinate the tempeh, slice the block of tempeh in half and slice each half lengthways so you have 4 thin fillets.

Combine the water, vinegar, lemon juice, 2 teaspoons of the Old Bay and 1 teaspoon each salt and pepper in a shallow dish and submerge the tempeh fillets in the marinade. Chill for at least 30 minutes or up to 6 hours. Do not leave them longer than that or they may be too soft to handle without breaking.

When you are ready to fry the tempeh, add vegetable oil to a heavy-based pot or deep fryer and heat to 180°C/350°F or as high as 182°C/360°F on a deep-frying thermometer.

To make the batter, put 30 g/1 oz of the flour in a bowl. In another bowl, combine the remaining 100 g/3½ oz flour, remaining teaspoon salt, remaining teaspoon Old Bay seasoning and remaining ½ teaspoon ground pepper with the baking powder and paprika. Leave out the beer until the oil is hot enough to fry.

Take each tempeh fillet from the marinade and dredge through the flour, getting all sides well coated.

CONTINUED

When you're ready to fry, gently stir the beer into the flour and spice mixture. Don't stir too much, as you want air in the batter.

Coat a fillet in the beer batter and put it directly into the hot oil. You'll probably need to do 1 fillet at a time so you don't overcrowd the pot. Cook for 2 minutes, flipping the fillet after 1 minute, until golden brown.

Using a slotted spoon, remove the fried tempeh fillet to a wire rack set over a baking sheet. This will help keep the fillets crispy while you continue frying. Laying them on kitchen paper could make the fillets soggy. Make sure the oil is still between 180°C/350°F and 182°C/365°F before frying another fillet.

To assemble the sandwiches, cut the buns in half and toast, if you like. Spread some tartar sauce on the bottom half of each bun, then add the sprouts, a fillet, avocado slices and more tartar sauce on top.

These are best consumed right after frying, but leftover fried fillets can be chilled and consumed within 4 – 5 days. Warm the fillets over a medium-high heat in a pan or in a preheated 190°C/375°F/Gas Mark 5 oven. However, they might not get as crispy as when you first fried them.

buffalo cauliflower sandwich

MAKES 4 sandwiches
PREP TIME 30 minutes
COOK TIME 50 minutes

prep ahead

The Classic Ranch (page 223)

breaded buffalo cauliflower

2 cauliflower heads

200 g/7 oz plain flour or gluten-free rice flour

4 teaspoons garlic powder

4 teaspoons onion powder

2 teaspoons ground cumin

2 teaspoons paprika

½ teaspoon sea salt

½ teaspoon ground pepper

175 ml/6 fl oz unsweetened non-dairy milk

175 ml/6 fl oz water

130 g/4½ oz panko-style breadcrumbs or gluten-free breadcrumbs

4 tablespoons vegan butter

350 ml/12 fl oz Tabasco buffalo-style hot sauce

sandwiches

4 bread rolls

The Classic Ranch

1 thinly sliced red onion (about 130 g/4½ oz) or Pickled Red Onions (page 107)

150 g/5½ oz shredded or finely chopped iceberg or leaf lettuce

2 tomatoes, thinly sliced

4 gherkins

It's our claim to fame. . . buffalo cauliflower. This recipe is the most visited page on the blog and the most watched YouTube video. Newcomers, feast your eyes on the buffalo cauliflower sandwich! You diehards will notice and recognize the revamp on the breading. I've added panko-style breadcrumbs 'cause it makes the cauliflower crispy and crunchy as hell. Not the kind of crunch that'll tear up the roof of your mouth, but the kind of crunch that'll definitely make you relapse and forget that you're biting into a piece of cauliflower. It makes a heck of a good replacement for chicken in this spicy stacked monster of a sandwich!

Preheat the oven to 230°C/450°F/Gas Mark 8. Line a baking sheet with non-stick baking paper. In this case, non-stick baking paper is absolutely necessary, or the cauliflower and batter will stick to the sheet.

To prepare the cauliflower, remove the leafy parts, being careful not to cut off any florets. Slice each head in half from the top. From the inside of each half, cut a slice 2 – 2.5 cm/¾ – 1 inch thick. You now have 4 large cauliflower cross-sections or steaks. You can reserve the remaining florets to make buffalo bites using the same batter and method or the Southern Fried Cauliflower (page 46), or you can roast them up for another meal.

Mix the flour, garlic powder, onion powder, cumin, paprika, salt, pepper, non-dairy milk and water together in a bowl until well combined. The amount of liquid or flour may need to be increased if you replace the plain flour with gluten-free flour. It should be thick enough that it doesn't pool too much around the steak.

Transfer the batter to a wide, shallow dish that will fit your cauliflower steaks. Place the breadcrumbs in another dish or large bowl. Immerse each steak in the batter, using one hand to coat all the crevices and letting just a bit of the excess drip back into the dish.

Coat all sides of the steaks in the breadcrumbs. Place the breaded cauliflower steaks on the baking sheet.

CONTINUED

Bake for 25 minutes, until crispy, flipping the steaks halfway through the bake time. If you go to flip the steaks and the batter feels stuck, it needs to bake longer on that side.

Just before the cauliflower finishes baking, melt the vegan butter and whisk it into the hot sauce in a shallow dish.

Remove the cauliflower from the oven. You may want to let the steaks cool slightly so you can handle them. You may need to replace the non-stick baking paper with a new sheet if it's really soaked through or burned quite a bit.

Coat the breaded cauliflower steaks evenly on all sides in the buffalo sauce. Reserve the excess sauce to baste the cauliflower before serving. Bake again for 25 minutes, flipping the steaks halfway through the bake time.

To assemble the sandwiches, just before the cauliflower is done baking, cut the rolls in half and toast, if you like. Spread a generous amount of ranch dressing on the cut sides of each roll. Place a buffalo cauliflower steak on the bottom half. Add the red onion slices, lettuce, tomato slices and then the top half of the roll. Serve with a gherkin or slice the gherkins and add to the sandwich.

hot tip You can slice leftover buffalo cauliflower steaks into breaded strips and make a salad with greens and veggies like tomatoes, cucumbers and red onion. Then drown it in ranch dressing. It's outstanding! You can also use half Tabasco buffalo-style hot sauce and half BBQ sauce for a milder version of this sandwich.

hot tip The best place to look for cans of jackfruit is in Asian supermarkets or Chinatown. If the fruit doesn't feel too soft and can't be shredded by hand easily right out of the can, you might have fruit that's nearly raw. It will need to be boiled for 20 – 30 minutes before cooking the way I've instructed to get it tender. Not all cans are created equal!

bbq jackfruit sandwich

MAKES 4 sandwiches
PREP TIME 50 minutes, plus
2 hours or overnight for pickling
COOK TIME 10 minutes

prep ahead

The Jalapeño-lime Aioli
(page 227)

The BBQ Sauce (page 209)

pickled red onions

1 large red onion

125 ml/4 fl oz white wine
vinegar

1 tablespoon sea salt

1 tablespoon granulated sugar

125 – 225 ml/4 – 8 fl oz water

slaw

180 g/6½ oz shredded or finely
chopped Chinese cabbage

50 g/1¾ oz baby spinach, finely
chopped

2 green onions, white and green
parts, finely chopped

2 tablespoons finely chopped
fresh mint

2 tablespoons finely chopped
fresh coriander

125 ml/4 fl oz The Jalapeño-
lime Aioli

Ground pepper

bbq jackfruit

2 cans young jackfruit in water
or brine (not syrup, see hot tip)

2 teaspoons vegetable oil

225 ml/8 fl oz The BBQ Sauce

Sea salt and ground pepper

sandwiches

4 ciabatta-style rolls

4 tablespoons The Jalapeño-
lime Aioli

A fruit that looks like meat? No you haven't fallen into an alternate universe! If you've never seen or heard of jackfruit, you'll be truly fooled and pleasantly surprised by this sandwich. While you could skip the pickled onions, they really add a nice element to the sandwich. You can also make this recipe even easier by using your favourite shop-bought BBQ sauce rather than our homemade version. I won't negotiate on that slaw though. The aroma from the fresh herbs and mix of textures when the cool creamy slaw meshes with the sweet and smoky jackfruit is perfect. If you're not drooling right now, you might want to check your pulse!

To make the pickled onions, thinly slice the onion with a mandolin. If you don't have one, use a sharp knife and slice the onions as thin as you can so you can see the knife through the slices. Combine the vinegar, sea salt and sugar in a glass bowl or large jar. Add the onions and fill with water to submerge and cover all the onions. Chill for as little as 2 hours, but overnight is best if you can prep ahead. Consume within 2 weeks.

To prepare the slaw, combine all the ingredients together in a bowl. Chill while you prepare the jackfruit.

To prepare the jackfruit, drain the jackfruit and rinse well. Squeeze out the excess liquid from the fruit through a sieve if the fruit seems excessively watery. Pat dry with kitchen paper.

Heat a pan over a medium heat with the vegetable oil and add the jackfruit, pulling it with your hands or breaking it up with a fork into shreds. Break up small bulbs or remove them if you prefer. Sauté for 5 – 6 minutes until lightly browned. Add the BBQ sauce. Turn the heat to medium-low and cook for another 4 – 5 minutes. Add salt and pepper to taste, if necessary.

To assemble the sandwiches, cut the rolls in half and toast, if you like. Spread a generous amount of aioli on both cut sides of each roll. Add slaw to the bottom half, then a generous amount of jackfruit and top with pickled onions and the top half of the roll. Serve immediately while still warm.

Keep leftover jackfruit chilled for up to 5 days. Reheat the jackfruit in a microwave or sauté it in a pan for a few minutes until heated through.

monte cristo

MAKES 4 sandwiches
PREP TIME 20 minutes
COOK TIME 35 minutes

prep ahead

Tofu Bacon Slices (page 10)

ingredients

225 ml/8 fl oz unsweetened non-dairy milk

40 g/1½ oz chickpea flour

3 tablespoons nutritional yeast

2 tablespoons maple syrup

½ teaspoon sea salt

8 slices sourdough bread

4 tablespoons vegan butter, for frying

2 tablespoons Dijon mustard

2 tablespoons vegan mayonnaise

12 vegan provolone or Cheddar-style cheese slices

Tofu Bacon Slices

1 – 2 teaspoons icing sugar (optional)

75 g/2½ oz maple syrup or raspberry jam, to serve

If you don't know what a Monte Cristo is, it's basically a French toast grilled cheese sandwich traditionally made with ham, turkey and cheese in the middle. Oh, and sugar on top. . . because, America. Sounds kinda gross and kinda awesome all at the same time right? But one thing's for sure. . . this sandwich is a surefire hangover cure!

Combine the non-dairy milk, chickpea flour, nutritional yeast, maple syrup and salt in a wide, shallow dish. Place 2 slices of bread into the batter and allow the slices to sit in the batter for 1 – 2 minutes. Depending on the thickness and type of bread you're using, you might want to soak for more or less time. The slices should be well coated on both sides but not overly soggy.

Meanwhile, heat a large non-stick frying pan over a medium heat with 1 tablespoon of the vegan butter.

Place 2 battered slices of the bread in the pan and cook on one side for approximately 3 minutes. Flip and put Dijon mustard on 1 slice and vegan mayonnaise on the other. Use 3 slices of cheese per sandwich and divide between the 2 pieces of bread. Top 1 bread slice with a few pieces of the bacon slices. Continue to cook for 3 minutes, then put the two halves together to assemble the sandwich, lower the heat and cover the pan with a lid. The cheese should melt in another 2 minutes, but the heat should be low enough that the bread won't burn.

Repeat with the remaining sandwiches. Adjust the heat as you go and continue frying each sandwich, adding 1 tablespoon of the vegan butter to the pan for each one.

Top the finished sandwiches with icing sugar, if you like, and serve with maple syrup for dipping.

the ramen burger

MAKES 4 sandwiches
PREP TIME 20 minutes
COOK TIME 35 minutes

prep ahead

The Thousand Island (page 223) or The Spicy Sriracha Aioli (page 227)

The BBQ Sauce (page 209), optional

sandwiches

1 tablespoon oil

4 vegan burger patties, or 8 patties for a double decker

125 ml/4 fl oz The BBQ Sauce

4 vegan Cheddar cheese slices

125 ml/4 fl oz The Thousand Island or The Spicy Sriracha Aioli

150 g/5½ oz shredded lettuce

1 tomato, sliced thick

ramen patties

2 vegan onion or other bouillon cubes dissolved in 750 ml/1¼ pints water, or 750 ml/1¼ pints low-salt vegetable stock

4 (100 g/3½ oz) packs instant ramen noodles (vegan-friendly)

2 tablespoons vegetable oil, for frying

I ain't frontin'! This idea belongs right up there with a leaked Kardashian nude, a Bieber break-up, or anything Kanye tweets. It's a tad stunty, but I had to, 'cause it's friggin' delicious! The ramen burger would fit in at a birthday bash, kegger or potluck, or maybe one of those Friday nights when you just want to impress yourself and your dog. This sandwich is a bit of a messy one, and you will not look good eating it. But I dare you to take a walk where the wild things are, and if you make this please send noods to @hotforfood.

To make the sandwiches, heat the oil in a frying pan over medium heat and cook the burger patties for about 3 minutes on each side or until lightly charred. Then coat one cooked side with the BBQ sauce, flip, coat the other side and cook for a further 3 minutes. Flip, place a Cheddar slice on top and cook for 3 more minutes. Lower the heat or turn off the heat and cover the pan to keep the patties warm and continue melting the cheese.

Meanwhile, prepare the ramen patties. Bring the stock to the boil. Add the noodles and cook for 3 minutes. You could also use the instant ramen flavour packet instead of bouillon or stock. Drain the ramen but do not rinse.

Heat a non-stick pan over a medium heat and add a coating of vegetable oil. Lightly coat 1 or 2 ring moulds, each 6 cm/2½ inches in diameter, with vegetable oil. Place the ring moulds in the pan. Fill each ring with ramen noodles to just below the top edge. Oil a spatula or spoon and use it to press and pack the noodles firmly in the rings while you cook them for 2 – 3 minutes. Flip the ring and again press the ramen patties down to cook the other side for approximately 2 minutes. Reduce the heat to medium-low as the pan gets hotter. Remove the cooked ramen patties to a wire rack and gently remove the rings. You might need to trim any stuck noodles, but don't pull them or the patty will unravel. Continue this process until you have 8 ramen patties. As long as the rings and the pan are oiled, there shouldn't be much unravelling.

To assemble the sandwiches, coat one side of each ramen patty with Thousand Island. Place a handful of lettuce on top, then add a burger patty with melted cheese, tomato and another drizzle of BBQ sauce, and top with a ramen patty.

oodles of noodles

I have a confession: if I could live on any of my recipes, it would definitely be a pasta dish. Talk about comfort! All pillowy, soft, silky and creamy. Yeah, that's luxury! I wanted to triple this chapter but I had to control myself. My pasta cravings are real and frequent. So can we just stop it with the pasta shaming? When you want pasta, eat pasta. Cause YOLO! Anyone who attempts to talk you out of eating pasta isn't a real friend. Rant over. In this chapter you can work your way from novice to expert, starting with some of the über-simple ideas like the Spicy Peanut Noodles (page 121) or Green Pea Pesto Linguine (page 122), and when you finally master The Best Vegan Ramen (page 132), you basically win at life.

mushroom fettuccine alfredo

SERVES 4 – 6
PREP TIME 30 minutes
COOK TIME 25 minutes

prep ahead

The Parm (page 207)

ingredients

450 g/1 lb fettuccine

180 g/6½ oz raw cashews,
soaked in hot water for
20 minutes

225 ml/8 fl oz water

1 teaspoon apple cider vinegar

1 tablespoon freshly squeezed
lemon juice, plus 1 –
2 teaspoons (optional)

1 finely chopped onion (about
115 g/4 oz)

2 tablespoons olive oil

2 large portobello mushrooms,
thinly sliced

240 g/8½ oz thinly sliced
chestnut mushrooms

4 garlic cloves, very finely
chopped

½ – 1 teaspoon sea salt,
plus more for seasoning

½ teaspoon ground pepper,
plus extra for seasoning

125 ml/4 fl oz dry white wine or
low-salt vegetable stock

2 tablespoons finely chopped
fresh basil

1 teaspoon dried parsley

200 g/7 oz baby spinach

225 ml/8 fl oz low-salt
vegetable stock

4 tablespoons The Parm

Here's a classic no one ever thinks could possibly be re-created without butter and double cream. But it can be done, and this one won't weigh you down for days with loads of dairy. So say hello to the creamiest-ever vegan fettuccine Alfredo! If you're a mushroom hater, I don't understand your life, but you can leave them out. The wine, however, is non-negotiable. Okay, if you have to omit it I've got you covered below. Oh, and if you're allergic to nuts, just replace the cashews with the same measurement of soft tofu and use 125 ml/4 fl oz water when blending. Okay, no more excuses. . . get cooking!

Bring a large pot of salted water to the boil. Cook the pasta until al dente. Drain, but do not rinse.

Meanwhile, drain and rinse the cashews and add to a high-powered blender along with the water, vinegar and 1 tablespoon lemon juice. Blend until very smooth.

In a large pan over a medium heat, sauté the onion in the olive oil for 2 minutes until just softened. Add the mushrooms and cook for 4 minutes. When mushrooms are half cooked and start to release some moisture, stir in the garlic, salt and pepper and cook for 3 – 4 minutes.

Once the mushrooms have shrunk and released most of their moisture, add the white wine. Add the 1 – 2 teaspoons lemon juice if using stock in place of the wine. Simmer for 7 minutes until most of the liquid has reduced. Reduce the heat to medium-low, stir in the basil and parsley and cook for another minute. Stir in the cashew cream and spinach, and slowly stir in the stock. Cook for about 4 minutes until the spinach is wilted and soft but still bright green.

Add the pasta to the pan and toss to combine everything well. Cook for 3 minutes.

Serve immediately and add The Parm on top and ground pepper and salt to taste. If reheating leftovers, heat in a pan and add small amounts of vegetable stock while tossing the pasta to thin out the sauce. Chill any leftovers and consume within 5 days.

cold cucumber-chilli noodles

SERVES 4 – 6
PREP TIME 20 minutes
COOK TIME 6 – 8 minutes

ingredients

450 g/1 lb thick flat rice noodles

2 cucumbers

2 spring onions, white and green parts, finely sliced diagonally

2 tablespoons toasted sesame oil

2 tablespoons sesame seeds

¼ – ½ teaspoon sea salt

4 tablespoons chilli oil

I tend to add megaflavour to everything I cook, but in this dish I embrace the minimalist trend and really like the simplicity of salad onions with spice, sesame, salt and refreshing crunchy cucumber. It was inspired by something I ate a couple of years ago at Xi'an Famous Foods in Brooklyn. A friend claimed this menu item, known as A-1, was her favourite thing ever, which I mistook for hyperbole. But I was curious. Well, after ordering it and taking one bite, I was in love and certainly wasn't prepared for a long-distance relationship with this noodle dish so I made my own version!

Bring a large pot of salted water to the boil. If your rice noodles already contain salt, do not add salt to the water. Cook the noodles until al dente, approximately 6 minutes.

Meanwhile, cut the cucumber into ribbons using a vegetable peeler or slice very thin using a mandolin.

Drain the noodles, rinse under cool water and place in a large bowl. Toss with the cucumber ribbons, salad onions, sesame oil, sesame seeds (reserving 1 teaspoon for garnish) and ¼teaspoon of the salt (more to taste, if necessary). Divide among serving plates.

Drizzle each portion with 1 tablespoon of the chilli oil (or use more sesame oil if you don't want spice) and garnish with the remaining sesame seeds. You can also toss the noodles in only the sesame oil, salt and sesame seeds, leaving the cucumber ribbons and spring onions to place on top of the noodles in each serving. I think this looks prettier!

If you have leftovers, soften the noodles by heating them with a bit of water in a covered pan or heat in a microwave. Drain any excess water before serving.

creamy rosé penne

SERVES 4 – 6
COOK TIME 20 minutes

prep ahead

The Rosé Sauce (page 216)

The Parm (page 207)

ingredients

450 g/1 lb penne

1.2 – 1.4 litres/2 –2½ pints The Rosé Sauce

8 tablespoons The Parm

1 – 2 teaspoons chilli flakes (optional)

Sea salt and ground pepper

As elaborate and varied as pasta dishes can be, sometimes you just want to channel your inner college kid and eat pasta with tomato sauce. Our rich rosé sauce on penne is a splendid solution for easy weeknight dinners. But if you're looking to beef this up, you could add steamed vegetables, sautéed vegan beef-style ground mince or Tofu Bacon Crumbles (page 10).

Bring a pot of salted water to the boil and cook the pasta until al dente. Drain but don't rinse.

Add the pasta back to the pot you cooked it in and place over a low heat. Add 1 –2 litres/1¾ – 2 pints of the sauce (or more if desired). Stir to coat evenly and heat through for 3 – 4 minutes. Stir in 4 tablespoons of The Parm.

Top each serving with a bit more sauce, if you like, as well as more of The Parm, the chilli flakes, and salt and pepper to taste.

spicy peanut noodles

SERVES 4 – 6
PREP TIME 30 minutes
COOK TIME 15 minutes

prep ahead

The Spicy Peanut Sauce
(page 215)

ingredients

450 g/1 lb linguine, spaghetti
or flat rice noodles

2 tablespoons vegetable oil

1 thinly sliced onion (about
130 g/4½ oz)

3 spring onions, white and green
parts, finely sliced diagonally

2 garlic cloves, very finely
chopped

1 or more red bird's-eye chillies,
seeded and finely chopped

1 teaspoon very finely chopped
fresh ginger

1 thinly sliced red pepper
(about 75 g/2¾ oz)

1 broccoli crown, cut into florets

100 g/3½ oz mangetout

225 ml/8 fl oz The Spicy Peanut
Sauce

½ – 1 teaspoon sea salt

10 g/¼ oz fresh coriander
leaves, roughly chopped,
to garnish

45 g/1½ oz salted roasted
peanuts, coarsely chopped,
to garnish

1 lime, cut into wedges,
to garnish

You know those lazy nights when you want to order a takeaway? For me, I usually crave some kind of Thai noodles or curry. But they're seriously never as good as I imagine they're going to be when I ravenously place the order and it takes 45 minutes to show up on my doorstep! I know, first world problems. But the moral of the story is if you want something done right, you have to do it yourself. These noodles are just what you're craving, and you'll be slurping them up in 30 minutes or less, no tip required.

Bring a pot of salted water to the boil and cook the pasta or noodles until al dente. Drain, but do not rinse.

Meanwhile, heat a large frying pan or wok with the vegetable oil over a medium-high heat. Once the pan is hot, add the sliced onion and the white parts of the salad onion (reserving the green parts for garnish) and sauté for 2 – 3 minutes until just softened.

Add the garlic, chillies to taste and ginger and sauté for 2 minutes until soft and fragrant. Lower the heat slightly if the mixture starts to burn.

Add the pepper and sauté for 2 minutes until just softened.

Add the broccoli florets and mangetout and sauté for 6 minutes until about half cooked, but still bright green.

Add half of the peanut sauce and toss to coat well. Toss in the cooked pasta or noodles and the remaining sauce. Lower the heat, toss to coat thoroughly, and heat through. At this point, you can add ½ – 1 teaspoon of the salt to taste.

Serve immediately, as the pasta or noodles start to get slightly sticky the longer they sit. Garnish with the coriander, peanuts, remaining spring onions and lime wedges.

Leftovers can be reheated in a pan over a medium heat with a bit of water, or a combination of coconut milk and water, to loosen the pasta or noodles and sauce. Consume leftovers within 5 – 7 days.

green pea pesto linguine

SERVES 4
PREP TIME 20 minutes
COOK TIME 12 minutes

prep ahead

The Parm (page 207)

ingredients

450 g/1 lb linguine

310 g/10½ oz fresh or frozen peas

1 teaspoon sea salt

50 g/1¾ oz fresh basil leaves, plus extra to garnish

2 garlic cloves

8 tablespoons The Parm

4 tablespoons freshly squeezed lemon juice

4 tablespoons olive oil

Ground pepper

I love this pesto! It's made in 10 minutes, hides my vegetables in a pile of cheesy garlicky stuff and can even become a dip for crackers and veggies. This is my ultimate reduce, reuse and recycle food! But as multipurpose as this pesto is, it's still most epic served on pasta, and it certainly ain't picky about the shape. I just thought linguine needed to join the party for this one. Feel free to use whatever you have lying around.

Bring a large pot of salted water to the boil. Cook the linguine until al dente and add 155 g/5⅓ oz of the peas to the water in the last minute of cooking. Drain, but do not rinse.

While the pasta is cooking, combine the remaining 155 g/5⅓ oz peas (thawed and drained of excess water, if frozen), salt, 50 g/1¾ oz basil leaves, garlic, 4 tablespoons of The Parm, lemon juice and olive oil in a food processor until well combined and smooth but textured.

Place the drained pasta and peas back in the pot while it's still warm. Add three-quarters of the pesto and toss to combine well.

Serve the pasta with an extra dollop of pesto on top. Garnish with the remainder of The Parm, ground pepper to taste and basil leaves.

aubergine parm & spaghetti

SERVES 4
PREP TIME 50 minutes
COOK TIME 30 – 40 minutes

prep ahead

The Red Sauce (page 216)

The Parm (page 207)

cheese sauce

1 large aubergine

1½ teaspoons sea salt

1 teaspoon plus
1 tablespoon olive oil

175 ml/6 fl oz unsweetened
non-dairy milk

1 tablespoon tapioca flour

1 teaspoon nutritional yeast

½ teaspoon garlic powder

¼ teaspoon onion powder

¼ teaspoon ground white pepper

2 teaspoons fresh lemon juice

saucy spaghetti

450 g/1 lb spaghetti

1.2 – 1.4 litres/2 – 2½ pints The
Red Sauce

fried eggplant

475 ml/16 fl oz vegetable oil,
for frying

60 g/2½ oz breadcrumbs

8 tablespoons The Parm

1 teaspoon garlic powder

1 teaspoon dried oregano

1 teaspoon dried basil

¼ teaspoon sea salt

¼ teaspoon ground pepper

65 g/2¼ oz plain flour

125 ml/4 fl oz unsweetened
non-dairy milk

All plants are created equal. . . except the aubergine. The aubergine is like that certain someone who hasn't updated his or her hairdo since the '80s. Out of touch! And aubergine parm is the dish that EVERYONE thinks you eat as a vegetarian/vegan. Every time someone at a dinner says, 'Don't worry I made something for you,' it's either quinoa or aubergine parm. Clearly I've been the guest at these dinner parties far too many times, which is why you won't find quinoa anywhere near these pages and why my aubergine parm has been given a serious makeover. If you deep-fry anything, smother it in homemade tomato sauce and serve it with pasta, well, now it's palatable. This dish has a new 'do and it's ready for date night!

To make the cheese sauce, trim the stem and a small part of the base of the aubergine. Peel the entire aubergine, if you like. I like leaving the skin on for colour, but it's a personal preference. Cut eight 1cm/½ inch thick slices from the large base of the aubergine, these will be the aubergine parm rounds. Peel the remaining aubergine if you didn't peel the whole thing and cut into 5 or 6 slices of the same thickness. These slices will be used for making the cheese sauce.

Lay all the slices on wire racks or place in a colander and sprinkle on both sides with 1 teaspoon of the salt. Leave the aubergine to stand for 20 minutes to release moisture. Gently squeeze excess moisture out by pressing each slice with a clean towel or kitchen paper.

Sauté the 5 or 6 smaller slices for the cheese sauce in a frying pan in the 1 teaspoon olive oil over a medium heat for 4 – 5 minutes until very soft, lightly browned and completely cooked through. Remove from the pan and add to a high-powered blender with the 1 tablespoon olive oil, the remaining ½ teaspoon salt and the remaining ingredients. Blend until very smooth. Adjust the salt to taste, if necessary.

Meanwhile, to start preparing the saucy spaghetti, bring a large pot of salted water to the boil and cook the spaghetti until al dente. Drain, but do not rinse.

CONTINUED

garnishes

Fresh finely chopped basil, to garnish (optional)

The Parm

Ground pepper

To fry the remaining aubergine slices, add the vegetable oil to a large cast-iron frying pan to a depth of 1 cm/½ inch. Heat to a temperature of 182°C – 190°C/365°F – 375°F on a deep-frying thermometer.

In a shallow dish, combine the breadcrumbs, The Parm, garlic powder, oregano, basil, salt and pepper. Put the flour and non-dairy milk in separate bowls.

Coat an aubergine slice in the flour, next in the non-dairy milk and then in the breadcrumb mixture, using your hands to coat it well on all sides and edges.

Fry the breaded aubergine in 2 batches (depending on the size of your pan, but don't overcrowd the slices) for 3 – 4 minutes, flipping halfway through. Set aside on kitchen paper to soak up any excess oil.

Pour the cheese sauce into a saucepan and heat over a medium heat for 4 – 5 minutes, whisking or stirring frequently, allowing the sauce to thicken and become gooey like cheese. Turn off the heat and set aside.

Preheat the oven to grill. Place all the fried aubergine on a baking sheet and spoon about 2 tablespoons of the cheese sauce on each slice, spreading it out to the edges. Grill for 3 – 5 minutes until the cheese bubbles or browns on top. The timing may vary; watch closely so the cheese or aubergine breading don't burn.

Meanwhile, heat the sauce for the spaghetti in a saucepan over a low simmer.

Toss the spaghetti in the sauce while it's still simmering over a low heat.

Portion the spaghetti on to plates. Top each serving with 2 cheese-covered aubergine slices. Garnish with fresh basil, more parm and ground pepper to taste.

hot tip If you want to bake the breaded aubergine slices rather than fry them, line a baking sheet with non-stick baking paper. Place the slices on the sheet and spray with a light coating of oil (this will help with browning). Bake in a preheated 220°C/425°F/Gas Mark 7 oven for 30 – 40 minutes. Spread the cheese sauce on the slices and broil for 3 – 5 minutes until the cheese bubbles or browns.

butternut squash cannelloni

SERVES 4;
16 – 20 cannelloni
PREP TIME 45 minutes
COOK TIME 90 minutes

prep ahead

The Parm (page 207)

The Mozza (page 208)

roasted butternut squash

2 (90 g/2 lb) butternut squashes, peeled and diced

2 tablespoons olive oil

½ teaspoon sea salt

½ teaspoon ground pepper

béchamel sauce

50 g/1¾ oz soft tofu

250 ml/4 fl oz unsweetened non-dairy milk

225 ml/8 fl oz low-salt vegetable stock

2 tablespoons nutritional yeast

2 tablespoons tahini

1 teaspoon miso paste

2 teaspoons cornflour

½ teaspoon sea salt

1 shallot, very finely chopped

2 garlic cloves, very finely chopped

1 tablespoon finely chopped fresh sage

¼ teaspoon ground nutmeg

1 tablespoon olive oil

filling

100 g/3¼ oz soft tofu

Butternut squash is sexy. Wiki tells me she has alter egos in other parts of the world. In Australia and New Zealand she responds to the name butternut pumpkin. What a mysterious vixen! Wherever she goes, she's always the centre of attention whether puréed into a soup (page 86) or breaded and fried in our popular tacos (see hotforfoodblog.com). In this recipe she'll sweep you off your feet enveloped in cannelloni and a creamy béchamel that any nonna would approve of!

Preheat the oven to 220°C/425°F/Gas Mark 7.

To roast the squash, toss the diced squash in the olive oil, salt and pepper and arrange on a baking sheet. Bake for 25 minutes until the squash is golden brown, flipping halfway through the bake time.

Meanwhile, to prepare the béchamel sauce, combine the tofu, non-dairy milk, 125 ml/4 fl oz of the stock, nutritional yeast, tahini, miso paste, cornflour and salt in a blender until very smooth.

Heat a saucepan over a medium heat and sauté the shallot, garlic, sage and nutmeg in the olive oil for about 2 minutes until just softened and fragrant. Lower the heat if necessary to prevent the garlic from burning. Add the blended tofu mixture and bring to a low simmer, turning the heat back up if needed. As soon as the sauce starts to bubble, stir in the remaining 125 ml/4 fl oz of stock and bring to a simmer for 1 – 2 minutes until slightly thicker. Pour the sauce into a wide, shallow baking dish.

Once the butternut squash is roasted, turn the oven down to 180°C/350°F/Gas Mark 4. Reserve 115 g/4 oz of the squash and set aside.

To make the filling, place the remaining squash in a food processor with the filling ingredients and process until smooth.

To fill the cannelloni, transfer the filling to a ziplock bag and snip off a small piece of one corner. Very slowly squeeze the filling into each cannelloni, generously filling it. Arrange the filled cannelloni in 2 rows of 8 or 10 on top of the sauce in the baking dish, spaced 5 mm/¼ inch apart.

CONTINUED

175 g/6 oz The Parm

½ teaspoon ground nutmeg

¼ teaspoon sea salt

¼ teaspoon ground pepper

cannelloni

16 – 20 oven-ready cannelloni

300 g/10½ oz The Mozza

8 whole sage leaves

1 – 2 tablespoons The Parm

Ground pepper

Roughly chop the reserved butternut squash and arrange on top.

Distribute The Mozza over each row of cannelloni, allowing the ends of the cannelloni to be visible. Top with the sage leaves.

Cover the baking dish with foil and bake for 45 minutes.

Remove the foil and top the cannelloni with The Parm and pepper to taste. Bake for 15 – 20 minutes on the top rack of the oven until the sauce is golden brown. Watch closely so the topping doesn't burn. You may also need to grill the cannelloni for a few minutes to get The Mozza to brown on top. Serve immediately.

hot tip You can likely find pre-cut fresh or frozen butternut squash if you don't feel like getting intimate with whole squash. But if you use frozen pieces be sure to thaw them and drain any excess water.

bacon mac & cheese

SERVES 4 to 6
PREP TIME 45 minutes
COOK TIME 45 minutes

prep ahead

Mushroom Bacon (page 10), preferably made with shiitakes

The Parm (page 207)

pasta

345 g/12 oz elbow macaroni

topping

15 g/½ oz bread crumbs

1 tablespoon The Parm

1 teaspoon dried oregano

1 teaspoon dried basil

1 teaspoon sea salt

Mushroom Bacon

mac & cheese sauce

12 g/4¼ oz raw cashews, soaked in hot water for 20 minutes

285 ml/10 fl oz unsweetened non-dairy milk

90 ml/3 fl oz vegetable oil

15 g/½ oz nutritional yeast

4 tablespoons freshly squeezed lemon juice

3 tablespoons tomato purée

1½ tablespoons miso paste

2 teaspoons chilli powder

2 teaspoons onion powder

2 teaspoons garlic powder

2 teaspoons arrowroot or tapioca flour

1 teaspoon sea salt

½ teaspoon ground white pepper or black pepper

It's the best mac & cheese ever! Says anyone who's tried our classic version. Just a couple of tweaks and some smoky shiitake bacon thrown into the mix and we have ourselves a real winner! Anyone who knows me (in real life or online) knows that my obsession for mac & cheese is fierce, unrelenting and maybe even a bit of a problem. I dream about swimming in it! Hands down, I'm like a sommelier for vegan mac & cheese. So trust me on this one – don't mess with it. You'll be tempted to, 'cause I know you. But don't. Once you pour that cheese sauce in the frying pan, it will be near overflowing. You literally COULD swim in the frying pan there's that much cheese sauce. Don't omit any amount of it, unless you like disappointment.

Preheat the oven to 180°C/350°F/Gas Mark 4.

To cook the pasta, bring a pot of salted water to the boil. Cook the pasta until al dente. Drain, but do not rinse.

To prepare the topping, combine the breadcrumbs, The Parm, herbs and salt in a small bowl.

To make the sauce, drain and rinse the cashews. Add to a high-powered blender with the remaining ingredients and blend on high until very smooth.

In a 23 cm/9 inch cast-iron frying pan or baking dish, stir the pasta and sauce together until the macaroni is well coated. What looks like an excess amount of sauce will thicken during baking!

Sprinkle three-quarters of the breadcrumb mixture evenly on top. Sprinkle the bacon pieces liberally on top. Press them slightly into the breadcrumb layer but keep them still visible. Top with the remaining breadcrumbs.

Cover with foil and bake for 20 minutes.

Remove the foil and bake on the top rack of the oven for 10 minutes until the top is golden brown and the sides are bubbling slightly. Depending on your oven and the distribution of heat, you might want to set the frying pan under the grill for 5 minutes to get the top crispier instead of continuing to bake at 180°C/350°F/Gas Mark 4. Serve immediately. When reheating leftovers you may want to add more non-dairy milk to get it creamy once again.

the best vegan ramen

SERVES 4 (generously)
PREP TIME 45 minutes
COOK TIME 2 hours

prep ahead

Tofu Bacon Crumbles
(page 10), optional

broth

2 onions, halved

2 garlic bulbs

2 large sweet potatoes, diced

2 tablespoons vegetable oil

450 g/1 lb chestnut mushrooms

225 g/8 oz shiitake mushrooms

2 celery sticks, quartered

3 spring onions, quartered

2 thick slices of fresh ginger

½ head of Chinese cabbage, quartered

1 tablespoon sea salt

1 tablespoon ground pepper

1 large piece kombu seaweed

2.5 litres/5 pints extra water

tare

90 ml/3 fl oz low-salt tamari or soy sauce

75 g/2¾ oz tahini

2 tablespoons red or white miso paste

1 tablespoon seasoned rice vinegar or mirin

noodles & toppings

4 (100 g/3½ oz) packs vegan-friendly ramen noodles

1 carrot, grated or ribboned

140 g/5 oz frozen sweetcorn, thawed and drained

I'm half Japanese, but I'm not going to front like I'm some kind of ramen expert. I even read we stole it from China! Anyway this isn't a history lesson. You just want noodles drowning in a well-rounded, rich, layered umami broth. So I've created a homemade ramen that's less intimidating to make but just as decadent and flavourful as anything you'd order in a restaurant. And the best part, of course, is it's all veggie based! The tare is your main squeeze here. It's where all the flavour exists, bringing the salty, sweet, sour and spiciness to this dish or, rather, umami!

Some things to keep in mind: You'll need a large stockpot that can hold 6.8 litres/12 pints or more to make the broth. I've listed The Tofu Bacon Crumbles as optional, but they're like a fried pork substitute and are really tasty in this dish. The broth and tare can be made ahead and chilled – you will reheat the broth but do not heat the tare. The tare is meant to have hot liquid poured over it rather than being heated in the stockpot. If you heat it in the stockpot, it will separate and cloud rather than meshing nicely into the broth. This recipe is slightly more time-consuming than the others but certainly not difficult to make.

To make the broth, preheat the oven to 230°C/450°F/Gas Mark 8.

On a large baking sheet, arrange the onion halves, garlic bulbs and diced sweet potatoes. Roast for 40 minutes until the potatoes are cooked through and there is charring on the vegetables.

Heat the vegetable oil in a large stockpot over a medium heat and combine the mushrooms, celery, spring onions, ginger and cabbage. Add the roasted onion halves and 1 of the roasted garlic bulbs (smashing it a bit to release the roasted garlic). Sauté for 10 minutes until the vegetables are wilted and cooked down a little. Add the salt, pepper, kombu and water. Bring to the boil, then lower the heat, cover and simmer for 1 hour.

Meanwhile, combine the tare ingredients together until smooth and set aside. This can last in the fridge for up to 1 month but do not freeze it. It's best to make the tare as you need it.

4 spring onions, sliced
diagonally

225 g/8 oz warmed Tofu Bacon
(optional)

3 teaspoons chilli oil or sesame
oil (optional)

Strain the broth into a large bowl or another pot that can hold about 2.6 litres/2½ pints liquid. If you see any roasted garlic still intact, reserve the soft cloves, removing the skins. You can also reserve the mushrooms and add to the final bowls of ramen. Compost the strained the vegetables! Clean the stockpot and add the strained broth back in.

In a blender, combine 60 g/2¼ oz of the roasted sweet potatoes with 225 ml/8 fl oz of the strained broth, the roasted cloves from the remaining garlic bulb and any roasted cloves you pulled from the broth. Blend until smooth and cloudy. Then add this mixture to the stockpot of broth.

To cook the noodles, bring the finished broth to the boil in the stockpot. Add the noodles and lower the heat to a simmer. They will take about 3 minutes to cook. If you're not serving all the portions at the same time, only use the amount of broth and noodles you need. Alternatively, you can cook the ramen in a separate pot of boiling water. Drain but do not rinse. Then add them into the heated broth at serving. Store the remaining broth in the fridge and consume within 7 days or freeze for up to 2 months.

Traditionally bowls are warmed before serving. You can heat them in a microwave or, if they're ovenproof, in a 160°C/325°F/Gas Mark 3 oven for a few minutes, but it's not necessary. You can also reheat the remaining roasted sweet potato.

To serve, place 2 tablespoons of the tare in the bottom of each bowl. Top with 225 ml/8 fl oz of the broth. Stir with a chopstick to mix together. Fill with approximately 350 ml/12 fl oz of the broth, depending on the size of the bowl, and add a portion of noodles. Top each serving with shredded carrot, sweetcorn, spring onion, remaining sweet potato and bacon crumbles. Drizzle with chilli oil, if you like, or with sesame oil if you don't want spice.

the main event

Certainly anything in this book can be eaten as a main course because, again, there are no rules! But most cookbooks include a chapter highlighting 'meaty' main dishes. Well, here's my contribution in that department, and I think this is the perfect chapter to show off to people who are dumbfounded as to what a vegan eats. Just look at the variety of meals inspired by cuisines from all around the world. And I couldn't resist adding a deep-fried avocado, just 'cause! This is a great place to start if you're looking to adopt Meatless Mondays or need to switch up the usual dinner routine.

stuffed crust pizza

MAKES 8 – 10 slices
PREP TIME 30 minutes, plus
up to 1 hour for proofing
COOK TIME 35 minutes

prep ahead

That Dough (page 168)

Vegan Bangers (page 161)

ingredients

That Dough

2 – 3 tablespoons olive oil

460 g/16¼ oz grated vegan mozzarella

3 Vegan Bangers, pre-made vegan sausage, or vegan pepperoni, sliced

12 ml/4 fl oz pizza sauce

½ red onion, sliced

60 g/2¼ oz broccoli florets, finely chopped (about ½ crown)

½ teaspoon chilli flakes

Pizza with cheese-stuffed crust changed the world in the '90s, so why should now be any different? I honestly don't care what you put on this pizza or what you stuff inside the crust – just know that pizza crust always deserves your attention and that this one is begging to be stuffed. When I see people dispose of their pizza crust, I want to scream! That's the best part. So I figure stuffing it might entice you to see your slice through to the end, because it means you get a bonus surprise: more succulent bread and cheese. Oh, and if you're real sassy, you could always throw some Tofu Bacon Crumbles (page 10) in there too!

Preheat the oven to 245°C/475°F/Gas Mark 9.

For this recipe, you let the dough rise to double in size. Roll out the dough on a floured work surface to an 46 cm/18 inch circle. Transfer to a 40 cm/16 inch aerated pizza pan coated with some of the olive oil. The crust should hang off the edge of the pan. You can also place the dough on a pizza paddle if you're transferring it to a pizza stone in your oven.

Place 230 g/8 oz of the grated mozzarella around the edge of the dough and fold the dough over the cheese, lightly pressing it into the bottom of the pan to seal.

If you're using the bangers, brown the slices in a frying pan over a medium heat with a bit of the olive oil for 4 – 5 minutes.

Top the pizza with the sauce, brushing some onto the folded edge. Then top with 115 g/4 oz of the grated cheese and half of the onion, broccoli and bangers. Top with the remaining 115 g/4 oz grated mozzarella and the remaining onion, broccoli and bangers. Sprinkle with the chilli flakes. Brush the crust with a light coating of the remaining olive oil.

Bake for 20 minutes until the crust and bottom of the pizza are golden brown. Leave to rest for 10 minutes, then slice with a pizza cutter and serve.

loaded fries supreme

SERVES 2 as a main
or 4 as a starter
PREP TIME 30 minutes
COOK TIME 1 hour

prep ahead

Tofu Bacon Crumbles (page 10)

The Nacho Cheese (page 205)

The Soured Cream (page 210)

french fries

4 russet potatoes

4 tablespoons vegetable oil

1 teaspoon paprika

1 teaspoon sea salt

½ teaspoon ground pepper

toppings

The Nacho Cheese

12 ml/4 fl oz The Soured Cream

Tofu Bacon Crumbles

2 vine tomatoes, seeded and diced

1 tablespoon finely chopped chives

This isn't a mirage of fast food you can't eat! While it looks like a guilt-laden dish of french fries smothered with cheese, soured cream and bacon, it is – except it's made with simple plant-based ingredients so there's absolutely nothing to feel bad about. Have your fries plain or loaded to the max like this whenever the craving hits.

Preheat the oven to 220°C/425°F/Gas Mark 7.

To make the french fries, wash the potatoes and cut into approximately 1 cm/½ inch matchsticks, leaving the skin on. Place in a large pot of cold water and bring to the boil. Cook until you can just pierce the surface with a fork, 6 – 8 minutes. The potatoes shouldn't be too tender or soft.

Line 2 baking sheets with non-stick baking paper. Drain the water from the pot and toss the potatoes with the vegetable oil, paprika, salt and pepper until evenly coated. Lay them out on the baking sheets spaced 5 mm/¼ inch apart; do not overcrowd.

Bake for 45 – 50 minutes, flipping the fries halfway through the bake time, until golden brown and crisp.

Split the fries among serving plates, layering them with nacho cheese and soured cream. Top with the bacon crumbles, tomatoes and chives.

orange tofu & veggie fried rice

SERVES 4 – 6
PREP TIME 50 minutes
COOK TIME 45 minutes

fried rice

270 g/9½ oz long-grain white rice

600 ml/1 pint water

¾ teaspoon sea salt

2 tablespoons vegetable oil

2 spring onions, white and green parts, thinly sliced diagonally

2 garlic cloves, very finely chopped

½ finely chopped carrot (about 60 g/2¼ oz)

1 crown finely chopped broccoli florets (about 120 g/4¼ oz)

60 g/2¼ oz frozen peas

60 g/2¼ oz frozen sweetcorn

1 vegan chicken-flavoured bouillon cube dissolved in 3 tablespoons hot water, or 3 tablespoons low-salt vegetable stock

1 tablespoon low-salt tamari or soy sauce

¼ teaspoon ground pepper

orange sauce

1 tablespoon vegetable oil

2 garlic cloves, very finely chopped

2 teaspoons very finely chopped fresh ginger

2 spring onions, white parts only, finely chopped

¼ teaspoon chilli flakes

1 teaspoon grated orange zest

4 tablespoons freshly squeezed orange juice

4 tablespoons low-salt tamari or soy sauce

4 tablespoons unseasoned rice vinegar

When those Chinese food cravings come rolling in, turn to this page and stare at the photo before logging on to order a takeaway. Within seconds you'll realize that putting in the bit of effort it takes to make this simple crispy orange tofu and quick fried rice is completely worth it. It's mega tasty and fresh and a great way to fry up extra veggies you have lying around too.

To cook the rice, combine the rice, water and ½ teaspoon of the salt, cover and bring to the boil. Stir, cover again, lower the heat to a simmer and cook for 10 – 15 minutes. Adjust the water and cooking times to your particular brand of rice! You need 500 – 625 g/1 lb – 1 lb 6 oz cooked rice.

To make the orange sauce, in a saucepan, heat the vegetable oil over medium-low heat and sauté the garlic, ginger, salad onions and chilli flakes for 1 – 2 minutes. Add the orange zest and juice, tamari, vinegar, sugar and 225 ml/8 fl oz water. Bring to a simmer and cook for 10 minutes. In a small bowl, combine the cornflour and 1 tablespoon water into a paste and whisk into the sauce until thickened. Remove from the heat and set aside.

To make the fried tofu, drain the tofu and cut into bite-sized cubes. Allow the cubes to sit on a tea towel or kitchen paper to get rid of the excess water.

Heat the vegetable oil in a heavy-based pot or deep-fryer to a temperature of 182°C – 190°C/365°F – 375°F on a deep-frying thermometer. You'll need about 5 cm/2 inches of oil; the amount of oil may vary if using a deep fryer.

In a bowl, combine the rice flour, cornflour, salt, garlic powder and pepper. Do not add the sparkling water until the oil is ready. When you're ready to fry, fold the sparkling water into the flour mixture but do not overmix.

Using your hands, coat batches of the tofu cubes in the batter and delicately drop each one into the hot oil. Fry for 2 – 2½ minutes. If some stick together, gently separate them with a slotted spoon. Remove the

CONTINUED

100 g/3½ oz sugar

240 ml/8 fl oz plus 1 tablespoon water

1 tablespoon cornflour

Fried Tofu

2 blocks (450 g/16 oz each) medium-firm tofu

1 – 1.4 litres/1¾ – 2½ pints vegetable oil, for frying

135 g/4¾ oz brown rice flour

1 tablespoon cornflour

½ teaspoon sea salt

½ teaspoon garlic powder

¼ teaspoon ground pepper

225 ml/8 fl oz cold sparkling water

crispy tofu from the oil with the slotted spoon to kitchen paper to absorb excess oil. Continue this process to fry the remaining tofu cubes.

To finish the fried rice, heat a large frying pan or wok over a medium-high heat with the vegetable oil and sauté the spring onions (reserving some for a garnish), garlic, carrot, broccoli, peas and sweetcorn for 5 minutes until softened and slightly browned. Adjust the heat to avoid burning the garlic. Add the cooked rice, stock, tamari, pepper and remaining ¼ teaspoon salt. Continue cooking for 5 – 6 minutes, stirring occasionally, until the rice has some crispy parts and the vegetables are cooked but still bright in colour. You can cook the rice longer if you prefer.

Just before the rice is finished, heat the orange sauce to a simmer if it has cooled down. Remove it from the heat and pour into a bowl. Toss batches of the crispy tofu in the sauce, coating them evenly.

Garnish the tofu with the reserved salad onions and serve over the fried rice.

fried avocados with jackfruit

MAKES 6 servings, 12 pieces
PREP TIME 40 minutes
COOK TIME 45 minutes

prep ahead

The Classic Ranch (page 223)

beer-braised jackfruit

2 cans young jackfruit in water or brine (not syrup)

130 g/4½ oz thinly sliced onion (about 1 onion)

1 tablespoon vegetable oil

½ finely chopped red pepper (about 55 g/2 oz)

125 g/4½ oz finely chopped pineapple

2 teaspoons very finely chopped fresh ginger

2 garlic cloves, very finely chopped

½ teaspoon chilli flakes

Grated zest and juice of 1 lime

2 tablespoons vegan Worcestershire sauce

225 ml/8 fl oz vegan-friendly lager or ale or 225 ml/8 fl oz vegetable stock

fried avocados

1 – 1.4 litres/1¾ – 2½ pints vegetable oil, for deep-frying

100 g/3½ oz plain flour

225 ml/8 fl oz unsweetened non-dairy milk

90 g/3¼ oz breadcrumbs

1 teaspoon garlic powder

1 teaspoon chipotle chilli powder or chilli powder

This dish started out as a whole avocado stuffed and then deep-fried, which worked, but it really wasn't much to look at and was difficult to eat. But frying the halves of an avo and stuffing them with this delectable meaty jackfruit worked out much better. I have no idea what this is, except a fun dinner party or potluck idea to show off and gloat about how much of a kitchen wizard you are. The real skill is in timing the execution of this recipe so the ripeness of the avocados is perfect. . . not too hard and not too soft. If the avocados are too ripe and mushy, it won't work!

To make the beer-braised jackfruit, drain the jackfruit and rinse well. Squeeze out the excess liquid from the fruit through a sieve if the fruit seems excessively watery. Pat dry with kitchen paper.

Heat a cast-iron frying pan or pan over a medium heat and sauté the onion in the vegetable oil for 3 minutes until just softened. Add the pepper, pineapple, ginger, garlic and chilli flakes and sauté for 6 minutes.

Add the jackfruit and sauté for a futher 3 – 4 minutes until lightly browned.

Add the lime zest and juice, Worcestershire sauce and lager. Stir to combine and bring to a simmer. Once the mixture is bubbling, adjust the heat to medium-low, cover and cook for 20 minutes, stirring occasionally. Once most of the liquid is absorbed, turn off the heat but leave covered to stay warm.

To fry the avocados, heat the vegetable oil in a heavy-based pot or deep-fryer to a temperature of 182°C – 190°C/365°F – 375°F on a deep-frying thermometer.

Place the plain flour in a bowl and the non-dairy milk in another bowl. In a third bowl, combine the breadcrumbs, garlic powder, chipotle chilli powder, salt and cumin.

CONTINUED

1 teaspoon sea salt

½ teaspoon ground cumin

6 ripe but firm avocados

serve with

The Classic Ranch

1 handful fresh coriander, chopped (optional)

1 lime, cut into wedges (optional)

Cut each avocado in half. Remove the stone. Gently peel the skin from the halves. Carefully scoop a small amount of avocado from the centre of each half to create more of a bowl, leaving the sides intact.

Coat each avocado half in the plain flour, shaking off any excess, then immerse in the non-dairy milk. Toss in the breadcrumb mixture. Use your hands to gently press and pack on the crumb mixture so the entire half is well coated.

To avoid overcrowding the pot, fry 2 halves at a time for 2 minutes until golden brown. Remove with a slotted spoon or tongs, allowing any excess oil to drip off before placing the halves on a plate or baking sheet lined with kitchen paper.

To serve, scoop a generous portion of the jackfruit on top of each avocado half. Top with the ranch dressing. Add coriander and a drizzle of extra lime juice, if you like.

hot tip Nut-free folks can blend the verde sauce with the thick cream from the top of a can (400 ml/14 fl oz) of full-fat coconut milk instead of using cashews!

bean & cheese enchiladas verdes

SERVES 4
PREP TIME 50 minutes
COOK TIME 25 minutes

verde sauce

60 g/2¼ oz raw cashews, soaked in hot water for 20 minutes

350 ml/12 fl oz salsa verde

1 tablespoon freshly squeezed lime juice

10 g/¼ oz fresh coriander leaves (optional)

enchiladas

3 tablespoons plus 1 teaspoon vegetable oil

½ finely chopped onion (about 60 g/2¼ oz)

2 garlic cloves, very finely chopped

½ teaspoon chipotle chile powder

½ teaspoon chilli powder

½ teaspoon sea salt

¼ teaspoon ground pepper

140 g/5 oz frozen sweetcorn, thawed and drained

200 g/7 oz spinach

150 g/2½ oz cooked haricot beans or 425 g/15 oz canned haricot beans, rinsed and drained

175 g/6 oz grated vegan mozzarella

12 (15 cm/6 inch) corn tortillas

1 jalapeño chilli, thinly sliced and seeded

toppings

1 avocado, stoned, peeled, and diced

1 spring onion, white and green parts, finely chopped

Handful fresh coriander, roughly chopped, to garnish

Salsa verde, to serve

Lime wedges, to serve

If you're saucy like me, you'll adore these bean and cheese enchiladas! They're stuffed to the max and drenched in a spicy, creamy, fresh green sauce. Since dairy is no longer my deal, I'm always ready to party with cashews, and I'm obsessed with this sauce! Combining the silkiness of cashews with salsa verde puts these lil' rolls over the top!

To make the verde sauce, drain and rinse the cashews. Add to a high-powered blender along with the salsa verde, lime juice and coriander. Blend on high until very smooth. Set aside.

Preheat the oven to 190°C/375°F/Gas Mark 5. Lightly oil a rectangular baking dish about 30 x 20 cm/12 x 8 inches with 1 teaspoon of the vegetable oil.

To prepare the enchiladas, heat a frying pan over a medium heat with 1 tablespoon of the vegetable oil and sauté the onion and garlic for 2 minutes until just softened. Stir in the chipotle chilli powder, salt and pepper and cook for another minute. Add the sweetcorn and spinach and cook for about 2 minutes until the corn is cooked and the spinach is soft and wilted but still bright green. Stir in the beans and 115 g/4 oz grated mozzarella and cook for a further 2 minutes. Remove the filling from the pan to a dish and set aside.

Wipe out the pan and set over a medium-low heat. Coat the pan with another tablespoon vegetable oil and heat the tortillas in small batches for 1 – 2 minutes, flipping as needed. Add the remaining tablespoon of vegetable oil if necessary for the next batches to get the tortillas softened and lightly coated in oil.

Pour a small amount of the verde sauce into the bottom of the oiled baking dish, spreading it out to coat the base.

Place about 4 tablespoons on each tortilla, roll tightly and arrange seam side down in the dish. Make 2 rows of filled tortillas.

Pour the remaining verde sauce over the enchiladas and top with the remaining 60 g/2¼ oz of the grated mozzarella and the jalapeño slices. Bake for 15 minutes until the cheese has melted and the edges of the tortillas are just turning golden brown.

Top with the diced avocado, spring onion and coriander. Serve immediately with salsa verde and lime wedges!

bbq tofu and jalapeño-lime aioli slaw
from banh mi bowl (page 64)

guacamole (page 156)

when in doubt...
put it in a taco!

You know my motto! Rather than create yet another taco recipe, of which the blog has many, I figured you could take some inspo from this taco vision board. Tasty morsels and components from this book can easily be re-imagined into customized tacos whenever you damn please! Pair fillings from the Finger Foods (page 33), Veggie Sides & Big Salads (page 55), Stacked Sandwiches (page 90) and The Main Event (page 137) chapters with your fave sauces and go to town. See you next Taco Tuesday!

fajita sauté, guacamole and soured cream
from fajita fiesta bowls (page 156)

oyster mushrooms and thousand island from oyster mushroom po' boy (page 92)

the soured cream (page 210)

the nacho cheese (page 205)

jackfruit, slaw, and pickled red onions from bbq jackfruit sandwich (page 107)

sweet potato gnocchi

SERVES 6 – 8
PREP TIME 70 minutes
COOK TIME 50 minutes

prep ahead

The Parm (page 207)

ingredients

2 – 3 peeled, cubed sweet potatoes (about 900 g/2 lb)

2 teaspoons sea salt

⅛ teaspoon ground nutmeg

⅛ teaspoon ground cinnamon

200 – 260 g/7 – 9 oz plain flour

6 – 8 tablespoons olive oil

6 garlic cloves, very finely chopped

3 tablespoons finely chopped fresh sage

270 g/9½ oz stemmed, finely chopped cavolo nero

4 tablespoons freshly squeezed lemon juice

Ground pepper

The Parm

Just Google 'gnocchi,' and you'll find many many methods and rules for how it should be made and handled. When I decided to test it for this cookbook, it was so much easier than chefy types have led me to believe. The pros are on to something, though, with using a ricer or food mill, but you can get away with mashing your potatoes by hand. I'd say you better be in touch with your spirit guides for this one kids, 'cause you're going to be relying on some cosmic intuition to know when the dough has been handled just enough, has the perfect amount of flour and is ready to be made into soft pillowy morsels for your mouth. So it's a good thing I took pictures for you! It's honestly not as hard as you might think.

To make the dough, bring a pot of cold water with the cubed sweet potatoes and 1 teaspoon of the salt to the boil. Cook until a fork easily pierces the sweet potatoes, 8 – 10 minutes. Drain the potatoes well and leave to cool.

Pass the potatoes through a food mill or ricer on to a work surface. Or mash with a potato masher, being sure there are no big chunks of potato. You will need about 812 g/1 lb 12 oz mashed potatoes.

Sprinkle the potatoes with the nutmeg, cinnamon, remaining 1 teaspoon salt and 4½ oz of the flour. Using your hands and the help of a dough cutter or spatula, fold the mixture in overlapping layers a few times until most of the flour is mixed in.

Add 65 – 130 g/2¼ – 4½ oz of the remaining flour to the dough while folding but do not overmix or add too much flour. You should still see flour as you fold the dough the last couple of times. The dough should still feel fairly soft and resemble potato but be able to hold its shape. Shape the dough into a loaf and leave it to rest on a floured surface for 10 – 15 minutes.

CONTINUED

Flour another area of your work surface for cutting and shaping the gnocchi. Flour 2 baking sheets to hold the gnocchi.

Make sure your hands are generously floured. Flatten the dough into a 1 cm/½ inch thick rectangle approximately 15 x 23 cm/6 inches x 9 inches. Flour a sharp knife or a dough cutter and cut the rectangle lengthways into nine 2.5 cm/1 inch thick rows. Cut each row in half into strips. Roll out each strip into a rope about 2 cm/¾ inch in diameter. Cut crossways into small pieces just slightly wider than 1 cm/½ inch. You will have 140 – 160 pieces.

Place the pieces on the floured baking sheets and cover with tea towels. You should boil the gnocchi soon after making them, or you can freeze the uncooked gnocchi between layers of non-stick baking paper in airtight containers for up to 3 months. Cook the frozen gnocchi, without thawing, as directed below when ready to serve.

To cook the gnocchi, bring a pot of salted water to the boil. Place batches of the gnocchi in the boiling water. They will take 2 – 3 minutes to cook and will float to the top. Remove with a slotted spoon on to a large platter or place the batches directly in a hot frying pan to continue cooking.

While the gnocchi are boiling, heat a cast-iron frying pan or nonstick pan over medium-low heat with 1 tablespoon of olive oil. Sauté 1 or 2 cloves of the very finely chopped garlic, 2 teaspoons of the sage and a small handful of the kale for 1 – 2 minutes until the garlic is soft and fragrant and the kale has just started to wilt. Add a batch of the gnocchi and about 2 teaspoons of the lemon juice. Brown the gnocchi 3 – 4 minutes on each side. Remove to serving dishes, season with salt and pepper and top with The Parm to taste.

Cook the gnocchi in batches of 1 or 2 servings depending on the size of your pan, but don't overcrowd it. Add more olive oil to the pan to cook the next batches in the same fashion.

fajita fiesta bowls

SERVES 4
PREP TIME 35 minutes
COOK TIME 25 minutes

prep ahead

The Soured Cream (page 210)

salsa

170 g/6 oz finely diced tomato

30 g/1 oz chopped red onion

10 g/¼ oz chopped coriander

Juice of ½ lime

Sea salt and ground pepper

lime rice

270 g/9½ oz long-grain rice

475 ml/16 fl oz water

1 garlic clove, very finely chopped

½ teaspoon sea salt

Juice of ½ lime

10 g/½ oz chopped fresh coriander

fajita sauté

75 g/2¾ oz sliced red pepper

75 g/2¾ oz sliced green pepper

130 g/4½ oz sliced red onion

4 large portobello mushrooms, sliced

2 tablespoons vegetable oil

1 teaspoon chipotle chilli powder

1 teaspoon sea salt

½ teaspoon ground pepper

guacamole

1 large or 2 small ripe avocados

Juice of 1 lime

Sea salt and ground pepper

serve with

280 g/10 oz frozen sweetcorn, thawed and drained

The Soured Cream

Veggie fajitas are usually one of two options a vegan has to choose from at a non-vegan restaurant chain. But I've always loved them! I think I have an affinity for that hot sizzling frying pan that arrives at the table steaming up in my face. Since deconstructing is my thang, here's a fajita in bowl form that makes an easy lunch or dinner when you're having a busy week. Feel free to serve with tortillas just like typical fajitas if you're feelin' it, and you can definitely throw a side of refried beans in the mix too! Garnish with additional coriander, if you like.

To make the salsa, combine the tomato, onion, coriander, and lime juice in a bowl. Season to taste with salt and pepper. Chill until ready to serve.

To make the lime rice, combine the rice, water, garlic and salt in a pot, cover and bring to the boil. Stir, cover again, lower the heat to a simmer and cook for 10 – 15 minutes. While the rice is still warm, stir in the lime juice and coriander. Set aside and keep covered. Adjust the water and cooking time for your particular brand of rice!

To make the fajita sauté, in a frying pan over a medium-high heat, sauté the peppers, onion and portobellos with the vegetable oil for 3 minutes until the peppers and onions are just softened and the mushrooms are releasing moisture. Add the chipotle chilli powder, salt and pepper and continue cooking for 3 – 4 minutes until most of the liquid has evaporated or until cooked to your liking.

Make the guacamole right before assembling bowls. Halve and stone the avocados. Scoop the avocado flesh into a bowl and mash with the lime juice, salt and pepper to taste.

For each serving, place a bed of lime rice in a bowl. Top with the sautéed vegetables, sweetcorn, salsa and guacamole. Garnish with the soured cream.

waffle-topped cottage pie

SERVES 4
PREP TIME 45 minutes
COOK TIME 70 minutes

prep ahead

The Gravy (page 220), optional

mashed potatoes

900 g/2 lb potatoes, peeled and cubed

1 teaspoon sea salt

½ teaspoon ground pepper

⅛ teaspoon paprika

2 tablespoons finely chopped chives

filling

1 finely chopped onion (about 115 g/4 oz)

½ finely chopped carrot (about 60 g/2¼ oz)

2 tablespoons vegetable oil

2 garlic cloves, very finely chopped

1 teaspoon fresh thyme leaves

½ teaspoon ground sage

½ teaspoon sea salt

½ teaspoon ground pepper

325 g/11½ oz coarsely chopped chestnut mushrooms

2 tablespoons vegan Worcestershire sauce

2 teaspoons tomato purée

140 g/5 oz fresh or frozen sweetcorn

115 g/4 oz fresh or frozen peas

150 g/5½ oz cooked lentils, or 539 g/19 oz canned lentils, rinsed and drained

1 tablespoon cornflour

1 tablespoon water

I told you how life changing buying a waffle iron was, but if you have yet to throw mashed potatoes in there you're in for a sweet surprise. In fact you might never eat mashed potatoes the same way again! They taste a thousand times better when they crisp up and have little pockets to store pools of sauce or gravy. Not to mention, they're such an impeccable topping to modernize an old-fashioned cottage pie.

To make the mashed potatoes, bring a large pot of cold water with the potatoes to the boil. Cook until tender, 10 – 12 minutes. Drain the potatoes and mash in the pot with the salt, pepper and paprika. Fold in the chives. If you're not making waffles, you can use the mashed potatoes on individual servings or on top of a larger baking dish, but I would add some non-dairy milk and/or vegan butter or vegetable oil to make the mash smoother. However, it needs to be dry like this for crispy potato waffles.

Preheat the oven to 200°C/400°F/Gas Mark 6. For individual servings use four 8-ounce ramekins or an 20 cm/8 inch square baking dish for a single pie.

To make the filling, sauté the onion and carrot in a frying pan with the vegetable oil over a medium heat for 3 minutes until just softened. Add the garlic, thyme, sage, salt and pepper and continue to cook for 2 minutes.

Add the mushrooms and cook, stirring occasionally, for 5 minutes until just over halfway cooked.

Add the Worcestershire sauce, tomato purée, sweetcorn, peas and lentils and stir to coat well. Cook for about 3 minutes until the corn and peas are cooked through, but the peas are still bright green.

Mix the cornflour with the water to make a paste and add it along with the stock to the pan, stirring until well combined. Simmer for 3 – 4 minutes until the filling is thickened and only a small amount of excess liquid remains in the pan.

CONTINUED

225 ml/8 fl oz low-salt vegetable stock, or ½ vegan beef-flavoured bouillon cube dissolved in 225 ml/8 fl oz hot water

Topping

The Gravy, warmed

If using ramekins, place them on a baking sheet and portion the filling among the ramekins. If you're not making waffles, place the filling in the baking dish, the mashed potatoes on top and bake for 20 minutes until the top is golden brown and the filling is bubbling.

To cook the waffles, heat up your waffle iron and spray it with a light coating of oil. Use a heaped 245 g/8½ oz potatoes per waffle and cook for 7 – 8 minutes until golden brown and crispy. This amount will not fill the entire waffle iron but make a size reasonable to fit on top of the 10 – 12 cm/4 – 4½ inch wide ramekins. The time may vary, depending on the make of your waffle iron. Place the crispy potato waffles on a wire rack until all are done. Set a waffle on each ramekin and bake for 10 minutes. Serve immediately with warm gravy on top, if you like!

bangers & mash

SERVES 4; makes 8 sausages
PREP TIME 40 minutes, plus curing bangers overnight
COOK TIME 1 hour

prep ahead

The Gravy (page 220)

vegan bangers

1 sliced onion (about 130 g/4½ oz)

2 garlic cloves, very finely chopped

1 teaspoon fennel seeds

½ teaspoon chilli flakes

4 tablespoons vegetable oil

250 g/9 oz vital wheat gluten flour

120 g/4½ oz crumbled firm tofu

12 g/¼ oz nutritional yeast

1 teaspoon sea salt

1 teaspoon ground pepper

1 teaspoon smoked paprika

1 teaspoon ground mustard

1 tablespoon maple syrup

2 tablespoons low-salt tamari or soy sauce

1 tablespoon tomato purée

½ teaspoon liquid smoke

mashed potatoes

1.3 kg/3 lb potatoes, peeled and cubed

4 tablespoons vegan butter

125 ml/4 fl oz unsweetened non-dairy milk

1 teaspoon sea salt

1 teaspoon ground pepper

2 tablespoons finely chopped chives

These homemade seitan sausages that I Frankensteined have slightly different seasonings and texture than the Saved By Seitan (page 95) sandwich meat. They are basically identical to my favourite brand of vegan sausages. . . nah, they're better! Of course, I can't tell you what brand that is because #notsponsored. However, making these yourself is highly rewarding. You'll just need to let them sit overnight in the fridge so plan accordingly. We've added them on top of the Stuffed Crust Pizza (page 139), but you can make different sizes for hot dogs or breakfast sausages. Shape them longer and skinnier for hot dogs and grill or pan-fry them in BBQ sauce. For breakfast sausages, make small patties or smaller sausage links and pan-fry them in a light coating of maple syrup. It's a real sausage party here!

To make the bangers, preheat the oven to 180°C/350°F/Gas Mark 4.

In a frying pan over a medium heat, sauté the onion, garlic, fennel seed and chilli flakes in 1 tablespoon of the vegetable oil for 4 – 5 minutes until the onions are soft and translucent. Lower the heat as necessary to prevent the garlic from burning.

Add the onion mixture to a food processor along with the 2 tablespoons vegetable oil, 125 g/4½ oz of the vital wheat gluten, and the remaining ingredients. Process until mostly combined. Add the remaining 125 g/4½ oz of the vital wheat gluten and process until the dough forms a ball and is mostly combined. Place the dough on a work surface and knead 10 – 15 times until well combined.

Cut 8 pieces of foil approximately 25 x 30 cm/10 x 12 inches. Place a portion of the sausage dough in the centre of each piece of foil and form into a log shape approximately 4 cm/1½ inches wide and 12 cm/4½ inches long. Wrap tightly, twisting the ends in opposite directions to seal the foil firmly around the dough and shape it into a sausage.

Place all the wrapped sausages on a baking sheet spaced 2.5 cm/1 inch apart and bake for 30 minutes until they feel very firm to touch. Let cool for 20 – 30 minutes at room temperature. They might still

CONTINUED

serve with

The Gravy

175 g/6 oz frozen peas

be warm, but then chill them at least overnight. Chilling is absolutely necessary; otherwise the gluten will not activate and the sausage texture will not
be right!

Prepare the mashed potatoes just before serving. Bring a large pot of cold water with the potatoes to the boil. Cook until tender, 10 – 12 minutes. Drain and mash in the pot with the remaining ingredients.

Just before serving, heat up the gravy in a saucepan and thin out with water or vegetable stock if necessary.

To cook the bangers, heat a frying pan over a medium heat with the remaining 1 tablespoon of vegetable oil and pan-fry the sausages for 5 – 6 minutes until browned on all sides. Add about 4 tablespoons of the gravy to coat the sausages and cook for 1 more minute. You can add the peas at the end to cook through or steam them separately.

Plate the dish with a heaped mound of potatoes, 2 sausages, peas and more gravy on top. Serve immediately!

mushroom, leek & tomato risotto

SERVES 4 – 6
PREP TIME 25 minutes
COOK TIME 35 minutes

prep ahead

The Parm (page 207)

ingredients

3 vegan chicken-flavoured bouillon cubes dissolved in 1.4 litres/2½ pints hot water, or 1.4 litres/2½ pints low-salt vegetable stock

1 leek, halved and sliced thin

2 tablespoons vegan butter

225 g/8 oz button mushrooms

¼ teaspoon sea salt

¼ teaspoon ground pepper

2 tablespoons finely chopped sun-dried tomatoes

370 g/13 oz Arborio rice

225 ml/8 fl oz dry white wine

125 g/4½ oz The Parm, plus more for garnish

6 g/⅛ oz basil leaves, finely chopped, plus more to garnish

3 teaspoons freshly squeezed lemon juice

1 thinly sliced spring onion (green parts only), to garnish

Cooking is a form of meditation for me, and comfort food like risotto forces me (and you!) to be present for the whole process of bringing it to life. You gotta give it love from start to finish, so Instagram breaks are forbidden during this session, k? This risotto is creamy, super savoury and even cheesy. The Parm works its magic in this dish and meshes nicely with the sun-dried tomatoes, leek and cute button mushrooms. Now, take a deep breath in and go!

It's important that the stock for cooking the rice be hot, so heat it in a saucepan and have it ready to be ladled into the risotto as you go.

In a stockpot over a medium heat, sauté the leek in the butter for 2 – 3 minutes until just softened. Add the mushrooms and cook for a further 2 minutes. Add the salt and pepper and continue cooking for approximately 4 minutes.

Stir in the sun-dried tomatoes and rice. Stir constantly for 3 – 4 minutes to release the starch in the rice. Add the white wine and simmer, stirring constantly, for 3 – 4 minutes until most of the wine is absorbed.

Add 4 tablespoons of The Parm and stir until combined into the rice mixture. Add 225 ml/8 fl oz of the stock and stir constantly until mostly absorbed.

Add another 4 tablespoons of The Parm and another 225 ml/8 fl oz of the stock. Continue stirring constantly until the liquid is absorbed. Add 750 ml/1¼ pints of the stock, 225 ml/8 fl oz at a time, stirring constantly after each addition until the liquid is absorbed.

Stir in the 6 g/⅛ oz basil and the remaining 225 ml/8 fl oz stock and stir constantly until the liquid is absorbed. At this point, check your risotto. It shouldn't be too mushy and the rice should have a bit of a bite but still be tender. Turn off the heat and stir in the lemon juice.

Serve immediately with more of The Parm sprinkled on top. Garnish with the salad onion or more fresh basil. Season with ground pepper.

hot tip For nut-free folk, fold in 12 g/½ oz of nutritional yeast instead of using The Parm or use a vegan Parmesan product instead!

sweet things

I believe there's always room for dessert, especially (maybe only) when it's homemade. I really love baking for other people. Any occasion means I'm getting in the kitchen and messing up my apron with flour just for the joy of seeing someone else's face light up with surprise and elation. These desserts aren't fussy or pretending to be healthy. There are cakes, cookies, tarts, trifle, cheesecake, and more! This is how I bake. I want it to taste and feel exactly like dessert, not breakfast or a granola bar. So it's baking at its best with all the essentials: flour, sugar, butter, shortening, sprinkles, chocolate and everything in between.

that dough

MAKES dough for 12 twists,
1 stuffed pizza crust, 16 fritters,
or 12 rolls
PREP TIME 15 minutes

ingredients

400 g/14 oz plain flour

1 tablespoon granulated sugar

2 teaspoons quick-rise instant
yeast

1 teaspoon sea salt

1 tablespoon vegetable oil

350 ml/12 fl oz warm water
(49 – 54°C/120– 130°F)

Did I mention I love bread? Not sure. If you love it as well, this multipurpose quick-rise yeast dough is crucial for when you just need bread! This dough is used in each of the recipes listed below, but I can't wait to see what else you use it for too.

· Cheesy Pesto Bread Twists (page 41)
· Stuffed Crust Pizza (page 139)
· Apple Fritters (page 172)
· Cinnamon Rolls (page 171)

In a large bowl, combine the flour, sugar, yeast and salt.

Create a well in the middle of the dry ingredients and add the vegetable oil and the warm water.

Fold with a rubber spatula or wooden spoon until the dough comes together to form a sticky ball. Lightly flour a work surface and your hands and knead the dough 10 – 15 times. Use a light sprinkling of extra flour on the dough and your hands when it starts to stick. The final ball of dough should be slightly sticky and soft, but you can still handle it.

For most recipes, you'll let the dough rest on the work surface for 10 minutes covered with a tea towel. After the dough has rested, you can wrap it in plastic and chill or freeze it. If proceeding with a recipe, roll out and shape the dough as instructed in the recipe. Once shaped, the dough will require time to proof to double in size.

For recipes like the pizza crust or fritters, you'll let the dough rise to double in size first. After you've kneaded the dough and have the final ball, oil a bowl with 1 teaspoon vegetable oil. Any excess oil on your hands can be patted on to the ball of dough. Place the dough in the bowl and cover with a damp tea towel. Leave it to double in size in a warm, dark place. This could take 20 minutes to 1 hour, depending on your environment.

If using frozen dough, thaw it in the fridge overnight. Place the thawed dough in an oiled bowl, cover with a tea towel, set aside in a warm, dark place and let it warm up and proof to double in size before shaping and proceeding with the recipe.

hot tip Not all flour is created equal, so if you use a different type of flour, these measurements cannot guarantee the same results. You cannot overhandle this dough. Adding too much extra flour in the kneading process will make the dough tough. Add only light dustings while kneading and handling the dough to prevent it from sticking too much. You can chill or freeze the dough prior to using it. The only exception is for the Apple Fritters, as the dough retains too much moisture, and previously frozen dough will not deep-fry correctly.

cinnamon rolls

MAKES 12 rolls
PREP TIME 25 minutes, plus up to 1 hour for proofing
COOK TIME 35 minutes

prep ahead

That Dough (page 168)

rolls

That Dough

50 g/1¾ oz granulated sugar

50 g/1¾ oz brown sugar

1 tablespoon ground cinnamon

3 tablespoons vegan butter, melted

frosting

210 g/7¼ oz icing sugar

2 tablespoons vegan butter, softened to room temperature

1 teaspoon vanilla extract

2 tablespoons non-dairy milk

Pinch of seeds from a vanilla pod or vanilla powder (optional)

What's cosier than smelling fresh cinnamon rolls baking? Probably nothing except cuddling a baby panda, but that's never going to happen! Oooh I wish, I wish. Okay, anyway these soft billowy, gooey rolls layered with cinnamon and sugar are snuggle-worthy nonetheless and will leave you blissed out after just one bite!

For this recipe, the dough is rolled out after it has rested for 10 minutes.

To make the rolls, while the dough is resting, combine the sugars and cinnamon together in a bowl.

Lightly flour a work surface and roll out the dough to a rectangle approximately 46 x 30 cm/18 x 12 inches.

Brush most of the melted butter on the surface of the dough, leaving 2.5 cm/1 inch of one long side without butter or filling. Sprinkle the cinnamon-sugar filling evenly on top.

Starting opposite the uncovered edge, roll the dough into a tight log shape. Take a sharp knife and cut 12 rolls, each 4 cm/1½ inches wide.

Brush the small amount of excess melted butter inside a 23 x 23 cm/ 9 x 9 inch baking tin or a large cast-iron frying pan. Place the rolls in the tin/pan, leaving a bit of space between the rolls and between the rolls and the edges of the tin.pan. Cover the pan with plastic film and a tea towel and allow the rolls to rise until double in size in a warm, dark place. This could take 20 minutes to 1 hour depending on your environment. You can leave them overnight and bake in the morning. Do not refrigerate.

When ready to bake, preheat the oven to 180°C/350°F/Gas Mark 4. Bake for 30 – 35 minutes until the tops of the rolls are golden brown. Leave the rolls cool enough so that you can handle them.

To make the icing, combine the icing sugar, butter, vanilla extract, non-dairy milk and vanilla seeds in a bowl and mix with a hand mixer or whisk. Spread the icing over the rolls while still in the tin/pan or spread the icing on each cinnamon roll individually for serving.

The rolls are best served immediately. Any extras should be stored at room temperature in an airtight container. Leftovers are best served slightly warmed.

apple fritters

MAKES 16 fritters
PREP TIME 30 minutes, plus up to an hour for proofing
COOK TIME 30 minutes

prep ahead

That Dough (page 168)

fritters

That Dough

2 tablespoons vegan butter

200 g/7 oz peeled and diced apples (1 cm/½ inch pieces)

50 g/1¼ oz granulated sugar

½ teaspoon sea salt

1 teaspoon ground cinnamon

1 – 1.4 litres/1¾ – 2½ pints vegetable oil, for deep-frying

glaze

350 g/12 oz icing sugar

3 – 4 tablespoons non-dairy milk

2 teaspoons vanilla extract

When you're vegan you can't just waltz into a divey doughnut shop and take your pick. Admittedly that's one experience I miss, but I've learnt to make every comfort food I yearn for, and apple fritters are definitely at the top of that list! I need you to make these, and to encourage you even more, there are step-by-step photos on page 175 so success is guaranteed. It's a lot of fun making these fritters. You'll feel like a kid mucking with Play-Doh so dive in and get messy!

For this recipe, you'll let the dough rise to double in size before rolling it out and forming the fritters. It's important to make the dough fresh. Do not use dough that's been chilled or frozen.

To make the fritters, melt the butter in a pan over a medium heat. Add the apples, sugar, salt and cinnamon. Stir to combine and cook until the mixture is thick and syrupy, 6 – 8 minutes. Turn off the heat and leave to cool completely.

Place the ball of risen dough on a lightly floured work surface and lightly flour a rolling pin. Roll out the dough to 1 cm/½ inch thick, to an approximately 25 cm/10 inch square or 25 cm/10 inch circle. It doesn't have to be perfect.

Pour the apples and syrup on half of the dough. Fold the other half over the apples and pinch around the edges with your fingers to create a seal. Cut into 2.5 cm/1 inch rows in both directions to create a grid of pieces.

Lightly flour the grid and your hands and then smash all of this together to form a loaf shape, pushing any escaping apples into the dough. Take a lightly floured knife or dough cutter and cut the loaf on the diagonal 4 or 5 times and then crossways again from the other direction.

Now lightly flour this mess and your hands, and grab the dough and apple chunks and form gently into small mounds, smashing each together to seal in the apples as best you can. The mounds should be 5 – 6 cm/ 2 – 2½ inches in diameter. Place the mounds on 2 floured baking sheets, leaving space between them for rising.

CONTINUED

hot tip When baking or cooking apples, I often gravitate to Granny Smith for tartness but Gala, Braeburn, Pink Lady or whatever you have will work just fine.

Cover the baking sheets with plastic film and a tea towel and let the mounds rise to double in size in a warm, dark place. This could take 20 minutes and up to 1 hour depending on your environment.

When you are ready to fry the fritters, pour the oil into a deep pot. You need approximately 5 cm/2 inches of oil. Heat the oil to 182°C/360°F on a deep-frying thermometer. Set a wire rack on a baking sheet lined with kichen paper, for holding the finished fritters.

While the oil is heating, make the glaze. Combine all the ingredients together in a bowl. Adjust the sugar or non-dairy milk if necessary to create a smooth, runny glaze.

It's important to fry the fritters at 182°C – 185°C/360°F – 365°F. If the oil is any cooler, you will get soggy oily fritters; any hotter and they will cook too fast on the outside and harden.

If any apples seem to be falling off just push them into the dough or fold over any excess, but don't handle the fritters too much. Gently place 2 or 3 fritters in the hot oil, adjusting the temperature as needed. Fry for 1½ minutes on the first side, gently flip with a slotted spoon, and fry for 1½ minutes on the other side. You may lose a few apples, but you can fish them out with the spoon as they float off. Once the fritters are an even golden brown, lift each one with the spoon, letting any excess oil drip back into the pot. Place on a wire rack.

Make sure that the oil is at 182°C/360°F before frying more batches.

While the fritters are still warm, dip them into the glaze, allowing the excess to drip off, or gently brush them with the glaze. Place back on the wire rack. I find using a brush helps get an even amount of glaze all over the fritter as well as in any nooks and crannies. The fritters are best served immediately and should be consumed within the first 24 hours.

customizable cake

18- 20 cm

MAKES one 7- or 8-inch double layer cake or 12 cupcakes
PREP TIME 30 minutes
COOK TIME 15 minutes

chocolate cake

225 ml/8 fl oz soya milk

1 teaspoon apple cider vinegar

220 g/7¾ oz plain flour

1 teaspoon bicarbonate of soda

½ teaspoon baking soda

¼ teaspoon sea salt

35 g/1¼ oz Dutch-processed cocoa powder

150 g/5½ oz granulated sugar

90 ml/3 fl oz vegetable oil, or 70 g/2¼ oz coconut oil, melted

1 teaspoon vanilla extract

vanilla cake

225 ml/8 fl oz soya milk

1 teaspoon apple cider vinegar

260 g/9 oz plain flour

1 teaspoon baking powder

½ teaspoon bicarbonate of soda

¼ teaspoon sea salt

150g → ¾ cup granulated sugar

150 g/5½ oz vegetable oil, or 70 g/2¼ oz coconut oil, melted

1 teaspoon vanilla extract

Seeds of 1 vanilla pod or ¼ teaspoon vanilla powder

apple spice cake

225 ml/8 fl oz soya milk

1 teaspoon apple cider vinegar

260 g/9 oz plain flour

1 teaspoon baking powder

½ teaspoon bicarbonate of soda

¼ teaspoon sea salt

These four cake recipes will provide you with the framework and bad-assery for great vegan cakes or cupcakes. I've given you the exact amounts for these flavour variations, but if you want to experiment, make sure you have the same total amount of dry ingredients and wet ingredients and all should go smoothly! Spices, fruits, chocolate chips or nuts are extra additions that shouldn't mess things up, but no promises. Baking has rules after all, and I certainly don't know all of them. I find using soya milk provides the best results for these particular recipes, but if you can't have soya, substituting another non-dairy milk will be fine. You can even substitute apple sauce for the oil!

If you need to double a recipe to make a four-layer cake or two dozen cupcakes, you should still make one batch at a time as opposed to doubling the ingredients in the same bowl. Use 22½ cm/9 inch cake tins so the layers aren't too thick.

Preheat the oven to 180°C/350°F/Gas Mark 4.

If making a layer cake, generously oil or butter cake tins and then dust with an even coating of flour to help easily remove cake from the tins. If making cupcakes, insert paper cases in the holes of a standard muffin tin or use a silicon tray placed on a baking sheet if you prefer.

In a bowl, combine the soya milk and apple cider vinegar (include the lemon zest and juice if making the lemon cake). Set aside for 10 minutes.

In a large bowl, sift together the flour, baking powder, bicarbonate of soda, and salt. If making the chocolate cake, include the cocoa. If making the vanilla cake and using vanilla powder, sift it with the dry ingredients. For the apple spice cake, include the spices. Stir to combine well.

Once the soya milk mixture has thickened, combine it with the sugar, vegetable oil and vanilla extract. For the apple spice cake, add the molasses and grated apple. For the vanilla cake, add the vanilla seeds. Stir to combine well.

CONTINUED

1½ teaspoons ground cinnamon

½ teaspoon ground ginger

½ teaspoon ground allspice

150 g/5½ oz brown sugar

90 ml/3 fl oz vegetable oil,
or 67 g/2¼ oz coconut oil,
melted

1 teaspoon vanilla extract

1½ teaspoons black treacle

150 g/5½ oz peeled and grated
apple

85 g/3 oz pecans, finely
chopped (optional)

lemon cake

75 ml/6 fl oz soya milk

1 teaspoon apple cider vinegar

2 teaspoons grated lemon zest
and ¼ cup freshly squeezed
lemon juice

260 g/9 oz plain flour

1 teaspoon baking powder

½ teaspoon bicarbonate of soda

¼ teaspoon sea salt

150 g/5½ oz granulated sugar

90 g/3 fl oz vegetable oil, or
70 g/2¼ oz coconut oil, melted

1 teaspoon vanilla extract

Pour the liquid ingredients into the dry ingredients and fold with a spatula, scraping the edges a few times as you go until the batter is just combined. Do not overmix. Small lumps in the batter are fine, but you shouldn't see pockets of dry ingredients that aren't incorporated.

For the apple spice cake, you can add the pecans to the batter or you can add them later to the iced cake.

If making a cake, divide the batter between the prepared tins and spread out evenly with a spatula. Slightly shake the tin back and forth to even out the batter. If making cupcakes, divide batter evenly among the prepared muffin holes.

Bake the cakes or cupcakes on the same rack for 14 minutes and check if a cocktail stick inserted in the centre comes out clean at this point. They may be done at 14 minutes or depending on the thickness of the cakes it could take 15 – 18 minutes. Remove the cake tins on to wire racks and let cool for 10 minutes. To remove the cakes, place the wire rack on top of the cake tin and flip it upside down. Leavethe cakes to cool completely before icing and assembling. For cupcakes in paper cases you can lift them out of the muffin holes with a spatula immediately out of the oven and place on wire racks to cool completely before icing.

buttercream icings

MAKES icing for 1 double layer
cake or 12 cupcakes
PREP TIME 25 minutes

chocolate buttercream

225 g/8 oz vegan butter, cubed
and chilled

50 g/1¾ oz Dutch-processed
cocoa powder

2 teaspoons vanilla extract

2 – 3 tablespoons soya milk

700 – 800 g/1 lb 9 – 12 oz icing
sugar

vanilla buttercream

225 g/8 oz vegan butter, cubed
and chilled

2 teaspoons vanilla extract

Pinch of seeds from vanilla
pod or pinch of vanilla powder
(optional)

2 tablespoons soya milk

800 g/1 lb 12 oz icing sugar

maple buttercream

225 g/8 oz vegan butter, cubed
and chilled

75 g/2¾ oz maple syrup, or
2 teaspoons maple extract

1 tablespoon soya milk (if
using maple syrup), or 2 –
3 tablespoons soya milk (if
using extract)

800 g/1 lb 12 oz icing sugar

raspberry buttercream

120 g/4¼ oz frozen raspberries,
thawed

225 g/8 oz vegan butter, cubed
and chilled

2 teaspoons vanilla extract

800 g/1 lb 12 oz icing sugar

**Each of these icings makes enough to ice the middle and outside of
a double layer cake or a dozen cupcakes. If you need to double the
recipe, make one batch at a time. I find that using a food processor is
the fastest and easiest method. You can also use a hand mixer. The
key to a fluffy icing is starting with cold butter and whipping it, then
gradually adding the extra ingredients, soya milk and icing sugar until
the perfect consistency is achieved.**

For the raspberry buttercream, strain the thawed raspberries through
a fine-mesh sieve placed over a bowl, separating the juice from the
seeds. Discard the seeds and reserve approximately 3 tablespoons
raspberry juice. You will use the juice instead of the soya milk called for
in the other buttercreams.

Whisk the cold butter in a food processor or with a hand mixer until soft
and smooth.

Add the cocoa and vanilla extract if making the chocolate buttercream;
the vanilla extract and vanilla seeds if making the vanilla buttercream;
the maple syrup if making the maple buttercream; and the vanilla extract
if making the raspberry buttercream. Add 1 tablespoon of the soya milk
or raspberry juice depending on the version you're making, along with
200 g/7 oz of the icingsugar. Mix until smooth. Continue adding the sugar
and soya milk or juice until the buttercream is fluffy, soft and spreadable.

If not using the buttercream straight away, store at room temperature in
an airtight container or cover with plastic film. For storage longer than 24
hours, chill the buttercream; allow it to come to room temperature before
using. You might need to add a small amount of liquid to smooth out the
icing before spreading.

To ice a double layer cake, place the first cake layer bottom side down on
your serving tray or platter. Using an icing spatula, generously ice the top
surface out to the edges of the cake. The icing should be no more than
1.5 cm/⅜ inch thick. Place the second cake layer top side down so you
now have a flat surface for the top of the cake. Use the remaining icing
to ice the entire outside of the cake. Decorate as desired. Serve the same
day as baking and icing for best results. Leftovers can be stored in the
fridge or at room temperature for 2 – 3 days. If chilled, leave the cake to
sit at room temperature before consuming to take the chill off.

hot tip If you're making a four-layer cake, you can double the icing recipes. You can also experiment with naturally colouring your icing using beetroot powder, blue and green spirulina, matcha powder, turmeric or other fruit juices and purées.

tiramisu trifle

SERVES 8 – 10
PREP TIME 40 minutes, plus chilling mousse overnight and trifle for up to 6 hours
COOK TIME 5 minutes

prep ahead

Vanilla Cake (page 177)

chocolate mousse

240 g/8½ oz soft tofu (from one 350 g/ 12 oz block)

25 g/1 oz raw cacao powder

100 g/3½ oz granulated sugar

2 teaspoons cornflour

¼ teaspoon sea salt

whipped cream

3 (400 ml/14 fl oz) cans full-fat coconut milk, chilled overnight

1 teaspoon vanilla extract

100 g/3½ oz icing sugar

cake

2 (8 cm/7 inch) layers of Vanilla Cake

125 ml/4 fl oz hot water

2 tablespoons instant espresso powder

125 ml/4 fl oz cold water

4 tablespoons coffee liqueur

40 g/1½ oz raw cacao nibs or finely chopped dark chocolate

2 teaspoons raw cacao powder

Using a cake recipe, you can make a tasty layered trifle with any kind of fillings you like, but I thought transforming tiramisu into a giant messy pot of chocolate mousse, whipped cream and coffee liqueur–soaked vanilla cake seemed right up your (well, my) alley. If you want to eat trifle right, ask you're your grandma or auntie for an old-fashioned trifle dish. It's usually 15 – 17 cm/6 – 7 inches wide and 18 cm/7 inches deep. Then dig into these luscious layers with a big ol' spoon and throw your manners right out the window!

To make the chocolate mousse, combine the ingredients together in a blender until smooth. Pour into a saucepan and heat over a medium heat, whisking constantly for about 5 minutes until the mixture is thick like pudding. Place in a bowl and chill for at least 6 hours, or overnight.

To make the whipped cream, scoop the thick cream from the cans of coconut milk into a large glass bowl, making sure not to get any liquid in the mix. Beat with a hand mixer or in a stand mixer for 4 – 5 minutes until fluffy and smooth. Add the vanilla extract and then add the icing sugar a bit at a time while beating. Once all the sugar is added, beat for a further 1 – 2 minutes until fluffy and smooth.

To assemble the cake, trim the edges of the vanilla cake layers so they fit inside the trifle dish.

In a wide dish that can fit the diameter of the cake, combine the hot water with the instant espresso. Add the cold water and coffee liqueur. Stir to combine well. Using a fork or cocktail stick, prick holes about 5mm/ ¼ inch deep into both sides of each cake. Soak one cake at a time in the espresso mixture for 30 seconds to 1 minute on each side. Use your hands or a spoon to pour some of the espresso mixture over the edges of the cake.

Place one soaked cake in the trifle dish. Top with half of the chilled chocolate mousse and spread out in an even layer. Sprinkle half of the cacao nibs on the mousse. Top with a layer of whipped cream, spread it out to the edges of the dish. Repeat the layers with the remaining soaked cake, mousse, cacao nibs and whipped cream. Dust the top with cacao powder through a fine-mesh sieve or sifter. Chill for 4 hours. Before serving, allow the trifle to stand at room temperature for at least 20 minutes to take the chill off.

fudgy brownies

MAKES 9 large brownies
PREP TIME 25 minutes
COOK TIME 35 minutes

ingredients

2 tablespoons ground flaxseed

6 tablespoons water

130 g/4½ oz plain flour

35 g/1¼ oz cocoa powder

¼ teaspoon sea salt

115 g/4 oz vegan butter

115 g/4 oz vegan chocolate chips

150 g/5½ oz granulated sugar

1 teaspoon vanilla extract

50 g/1¾ oz cup walnuts, roughly chopped

Brownies come in all shapes, styles and textures. . . much like humans. But I'd take a tin full of these over social interaction any day. These are a dense, fudgy brownie – crunchy on the outside, soft in the middle. You can make them into squares as pictured or bake them in a mini muffin tin for brownie bites!

Preheat the oven to 180°C/350°F/Gas Mark 4. Line a 23 cm/9 inch square baking tin with parchment paper, allowing the paper to extend beyond opposite sides of the tin, for lifting out the finished brownies, or grease the pan with vegan butter.

In a small bowl, mix together the flaxseed and water. Set aside for 10 minutes to thicken.

Meanwhile, place the plain flour in a bowl. Sift the cocoa powder and salt into the flour and stir to combine well.

Melt the vegan butter in a small saucepan over a low heat. Remove from the heat, add 60 g/2¼ oz of the vegan chocolate chips and stir until they are completely melted and smooth.

Add the sugar and vanilla extract to the butter mixture and stir or whisk to combine. Add the butter mixture to the dry ingredients along with the flaxseed mixture, another 60 g/2¼ oz of the vegan chocolate chips and the walnuts. Fold together until combined. Scrape the batter into the prepared tin and spread it with a spatula in an even layer out to the edges of the baking tin.

Bake for 30 minutes until a cocktail stick inserted into the centre comes out clean.

Allow the brownies to cool in the tin on a wire rack before lifting out by the edges of baking paper or cutting into squares.

Store in an airtight container at room temperature and consume within 4 – 5 days.

hot tip You don't have to bake all the cookies at once. Freeze the extra cookie dough for later! Allow the dough to thaw at least halfway before portioning out the cookies and baking. Bake as directed.

oatmeal chocolate chunk cookies

MAKES 4 – 4½ dozen cookies
PREP TIME 30 minutes
COOK TIME 50 minutes

ingredients

1 tablespoon ground flaxseed

3 tablespoons water

270 g/9½ oz plain flour

1 teaspoon bicarbonate of soda

1 teaspoon baking powder

1 teaspoon ground cinnamon

½ teaspoon sea salt

225 g/8 oz vegan butter, at room temperature

200 g/7 oz brown sugar

200 g/7 oz granulated sugar

4 tablespoons non-dairy milk

2 teaspoons vanilla extract

190 g/6½ oz rolled oats (not quick cooking)

255 g/9 oz vegan chocolate chunks or chocolate chips

Cookies. They're the simplest and most delicious treat. But I do have a problem with cookies masquerading as health food. Why on earth would you compromise what you're really dying for? This is a rich, chewy cookie that is not healthy. It's just the way a good cookie should be. . . I betcha can't eat just one!

Preheat the oven to 180°C/350°F/Gas Mark 5. Line 2 baking sheets with parchment paper.

In a small bowl, mix together the ground flaxseed and water. Set aside for 10 minutes to thicken.

In a large bowl, combine the flour, bicabonate of soda, baking powder, cinnamon, and salt.

In another bowl, beat together the vegan butter and sugars with a hand mixer or in a stand mixer for 1 – 2 minutes until fluffy. Add the flax mixture, non-dairy milk and vanilla extract to the butter mixture and beat until smooth and fluffy, approximately 1 minute.

Add the wet ingredients to the dry ingredients and fold a few times until half combined. Add the rolled oats and 170 g/6 oz of the chocolate chunks. Continue folding until well combined.

Place slightly more than 1 tablespoon batter per cookie on the prepared baking sheets, allowing enough space between the cookies for them to double in size.

I like to use the remaining 85 g/3 oz chocolate chunks for the tops of the cookies. Place 1 or 2, or more, pieces on each cookie before baking. This way the chocolate chunks will be visible on top!

Bake one sheet at a time for 10 – 12 minutes. Place the other sheet with prepared cookies in the fridge. You can also place extra cookie dough in the fridge before preparing them for baking the next batches. Watch closely, as you don't want to overbake the cookies, otherwise they'll be crisp rather than chewy. They should be a light golden colour and not dark on the bottom or too dark around the edges.

Remove the cookies to wire racks as soon as they come out of the oven, using a spatula. Continue baking the cookies in batches.

Store the cookies between layers of non-stick baking paper in an airtight container at room temperature for up to 4 – 5 days.

baked blueberry cheesecake

SERVES 8 – 10
PREP TIME 30 minutes, plus at least 4 hours for chilling cheesecake
COOK TIME 55 minutes

crust

95 g/3¼ oz rolled oats (not quick cooking)

100 g/3½ oz brown sugar

½ teaspoon sea salt

2 tablespoons vegan butter, melted

filling

120 g/4¼ oz raw cashews, soaked in hot water for 20 minutes

120 g/4¼ oz soft tofu

225 g/8 oz vegan cream cheese

200 g/7 oz granulated sugar

¼ teaspoon grated lemon zest and 4 tablespoons freshly squeezed lemon juice

blueberry topping

150 g/5½ oz fresh or frozen blueberries

2 tablespoons freshly squeezed lemon juice

50 g/1¾ oz granulated sugar

Making a vegan cheesecake that is indistinguishable from a cheesecake made from actual cheese is no easy feat. But this is The One, guaranteed. Cherish it! I had all the biggest vegan sceptics I know try it just to be sure, and they didn't even realize it was vegan. You can serve this tangy, creamy cake with any kind of fruit compote you want, but I'll always have a soft spot for blueberries.

Preheat the oven to 180°C/350°F/Gas Mark 4.

To make the crust, in a food processor, pulse the rolled oats into a flour. This should be a very fine mixture with no large pieces of oats. Add the brown sugar, salt and melted butter and pulse until the mixture comes together. It should press together when you pinch it.

Press the mixture in an even layer into the bottom of a 18 cm/7 inch or 20 cm/8 inch springform tin. You can also press it into an 20 cm/ 8 inch square baking dish. You can line the dish with non-stick baking paper for easy removal or you can serve the baked cheesecake directly from the dish.

To make the filling, drain and rinse the cashews. Place in a high-powered blender with the remaining ingredients and blend until very smooth.

Pour the filling on top of the crust. Bake for 45 minutes until the edges of the cheesecake are light golden brown. The centre might look a bit soft, but it will firm up upon cooling.

Allow the cheesecake to cool completely. Chill it for at least 4 hours or overnight. Only once the cheesecake has chilled completely should you remove the sides of the springform tin. Leave the cake to sit at room temperature for at least 30 minutes before serving to remove the chill.

To make the topping, combine all the ingredients in a saucepan over medium heat. Simmer for 6 minutes. Leave to cool before serving over the cheesecake. There is enough blueberry compote to put a good portion on top of the cheesecake and have some extra to add to individual servings.

Store leftover cheesecake in the fridge for up to 7 days.

blackberry crumble bars

MAKES 16 bars
PREP TIME 40 minutes
COOK TIME 40 minutes

crust

200 g/7 oz plain flour

½ teaspoon sea salt

50 g/1¾ oz granulated sugar

50 g/1¾ oz brown sugar

115 g/4 oz cold vegan butter, cubed

blackberry filling

585 g/1 lb 5 oz fresh blackberries

2 tablespoons granulated sugar

2 tablespoons plain flour

1 tablespoon freshly squeezed lemon juice

crumble topping

70 g/2½ oz rolled oats (not quick cooking)

50 g/1¾ oz brown sugar

½ teaspoon ground cinnamon

3 tablespoons cold vegan butter, cubed

Fruit crumbles are the epitome of fast and rustic baking. Literally, you can't F them up! They're delicious, pretty healthy and easily customizable. Now, me being me, I kind of fancified the recipe into a delicate crumble bar, which is pretty, but you could very well blow off the bars and use the filling ingredients and topping (minus the crust stuff) for any quick fruit crisp you're craving! Just remember, adding vanilla ice cream is a must for devouring this dessert the right way.

Preheat the oven to 190°C/375°F/Gas Mark 5. Line a 20 cm/8 inch or 23 cm/9 inch square baking dish or tin with parchment paper, allowing the paper to extend beyond opposite sides of the tin, for lifting out the finished bars.

To make the crust, in a food processor, combine the flour, salt and sugars. Add the butter cubes while processing. Combine until the mixture is the texture of fine crumbs. Alternatively, you can combine the flour, salt and sugars in a bowl and cut in the cold butter with a pastry blender.

Reserve 300 g/11 oz of the crust mixture in another bowl to make the topping. Press the remaining mixture in an even layer into the bottom of the prepared tin. It should be very well pressed and solid. Bake for 12 minutes until the edges are just turning golden brown. Leave to cool completely.

Meanwhile, make the filling. In a bowl, toss the berries gently by hand with the remaining ingredients until well coated.

To make the topping, combine the reserved 300 g/11 oz crust mixture with the rolled oats, brown sugar and cinnamon in a bowl. Pinch the cubed butter by hand into the mixture until you have a crumble with small chunks of cold butter. Keep the topping in the fridge until ready to assemble.

Spread the blackberry filling on top of the cooled crust in an even layer with no gaps. If you have any extra blackberries, use them to fill any gaps. Top with the crumble topping in an even layer.

Bake for 25 minutes. For the best results, leave to cool completely before cutting the bars. Store in the fridge in an airtight container. They're best eaten within 2 days max.

classic apple pie

SERVES 6 to 8
PREP TIME 90 minutes, plus
35 minutes freezing dough and
crust, plus up to 6 hours to cool
before serving.
COOK TIME 70 minutes

filling

2 tablespoons cornflour

2 tablespoons water

800 g/1 lb 12 oz peeled and
thinly sliced Granny Smith
apples

1 tablespoon freshly squeezed
lemon juice

150 g/5½ oz brown sugar

1 teaspoon ground cinnamon

½ teaspoon ground nutmeg

½ teaspoon sea salt

pastry

260 g/9 oz plain flour

1 tablespoon granulated sugar

½ teaspoon sea salt

225 g/8 oz cold vegan butter,
cubed

125 ml/4 fl oz ice-cold water

Baking a pie is like beating the whole video game. You didn't think you could do it, and your hands hurt, but with enough hours of game time it was, like, the biggest achievement of your life. Luckily for you, I've done the legwork and will walk you through every step of the journey with secret tips along the way. Let's up the ante and bake some pie!

To make the filling, combine the cornflour and water into a paste in a small bowl and set aside. Toss the sliced apples with the lemon juice in a bowl to prevent them from browning. In a large saucepan over a medium heat, combine the sugar, cinnamon, nutmeg, salt and cornflour paste. Toss in the apples and stir until well coated. Heat the mixture, stirring constantly, to cook the apples and create a thick syrup, 8 – 10 minutes. Most of the water should evaporate, and the filling shouldn't be too runny. Allow the filling to cool.

To make the pastry, combine the flour, sugar and salt in a large bowl. Cut in the cubed butter with a pastry blender until a crumb-like texture is formed with pea-sized pieces of butter throughout. Create a well in the centre of the mixture and pour in the water. Fold the pastry together a few times with a spatula until just mixed but still crumbly. Do not overmix!

Portion half of the pastry on a large piece of plastic film. Lift the sides of the plastic over the pastry to bring it together and gently form a ball. Finish wrapping the pastry in the plastic and gently flatten into a thick disc. Do the same with the other half. Chill the pastry for at least 15 minutes before rolling out. You can also leave it up to 24 hours in the fridge, but it may need to stand at room temperature for 5 minutes to soften slightly before rolling out.

Have ready a 23 cm/9 inch pie tin. Flour the work surface, your hands, and a rolling pin and roll out one portion of the pastry to a round 3 – 4 mm/⅛ inch thick, stopping every couple of rolls to make sure the pastry isn't sticking. Gently lift the pastry and lightly flour again underneath as you go.

The pastry should be at least 7.5 cm/3 inches wider than your pie tin all around. Roll the pastry over the floured rolling pin, transfer it to the pie

CONTINUED

hot tip Feel free to get fancy with the pie lid, by cutting strips and basket weaving or just check instagram for all those fancy cut out pie toppings that I have no patience for.

tin, and roll it over the top of the pan. Gently press the pastry into the base and sides of the tin. Trim any excess, leaving at least a 1 cm/½ inch overhang for shrinkage when you bake. Prick the base and sides of the pastry with a fork. Freeze for 15 minutes.

To help prevent a soggy bottom, you will pre-bake the pastry. Preheat the oven to 220°C/425°F/Gas Mark 7. Cut a square of non-stick baking paper larger than the pie tin and place it in the pan so it covers the base and sides of the pastry. Fill about halfway to the top edge of the tin with any kind of dried bean. Bake for 12 minutes. Remove the non-stick baking paper and pie weights and bake for a further 2 – 3 minutes until the edges are just turning golden brown. Remove from the oven, leaving it in the pie tin to cool on a wire rack. Once the base is cooled roll out the pastry for the pie lid. Gently trim any excess from the edge of the pre-baked case with scissors so it meets the edge of the tin.

Flour the work surface, your hands and the rolling pin and roll out the remaining pastry to a round 3 – 4.75 mm/⅛ inch thick, stopping every couple of rolls to make sure the pastry isn't sticking. Gently lift the pastry and lightly flour underneath as you go.

Evenly fill the pre-baked bottom pastry case with the cooled apple filling. Roll the pastry over the rolling pin, and roll it over the filling. Trim excess overhang where necessary. Fold the pastry over and gently tuck under the bottom edge of the pastry case all the way around the edge of the pie tin. Use the tines of a fork to press the top into pastry case as an extra seal. Make a few slits in the centre of the top to vent the pie while baking.

Bake for 25 – 30 minutes. At this point, you'll likely notice that the edges are done and golden brown but the top is not. Cut a square of foil slightly wider than the pie. Cut out a circle in the centre that is roughly the circumference of the pie inside the pastry edge and discard. Place the foil cover on the pie to protect the edges and continue baking for 10 – 15 minutes. If at any point you need to cover the entire top with foil, do so but allow the pie to bake at least 40 – 45 minutes total.

Remove the pie from the oven and remove the foil. Let it rest in the pie tin on a wire rack for at least 4 – 6 hours before slicing. If you like a real juicy pie, go ahead and serve it after 1 – 2 hours but the slices may not hold together nicely. The pie is even better when left to stand overnight at room temperature. Once the pie has cooled, you can cover it loosely with foil. Chill any leftover pie and warm up leftovers before serving in a 180°C/350°F/Gas Mark 4 oven with a piece of foil loosely on top.

lemon meringue pie tarts

MAKES 18 tarts
PREP TIME 80 minutes,
plus 4 – 6 hours for chilling
COOK TIME 40 minutes

aqua faba meringue

125 ml/4 fl oz liquid from 1 can chickpeas, haricot or cannellini beans

¼ teaspoon vanilla extract

¼ teaspoon cream of tartar

6 tablespoons icing sugar

¼ teaspoon xanthan gum

pastry

260 g/9 oz plain flour

1 tablespoon granulated sugar

½ teaspoon sea salt

225 g/8 oz cold vegan butter, cubed

125 ml/4 fl oz ice-cold water

lemon curd filling

150 g/5½ oz granulated sugar

1 tablespoon tapioca flour

120 g/4½ oz soft tofu

1 tablespoon grated lemon zest and 2 tablespoons freshly squeezed lemon juice

½ teaspoon vanilla extract

⅛ teaspoon turmeric (optional, for colour)

A classic lemon meringue pie was always one of those things I just relegated to never being able to eat again as a vegan. . . until now! These tarts are extraordinary. The whipped peaks of meringue are made using aqua faba or bean water. Ever heard of it? Well it's one of the most revolutionary plant-based food trends. You can now make meringue from the liquid of cooked beans – it's so insane, I know! The aqua faba meringue contains all the same ingredients you'd use for egg whites, but after a lot of testing I found the only way to get the meringue to really firm up properly was to add a bit of xanthan gum. It's a thickening agent often used as the binder for flours in gluten-free baking. Feel free to replace the lemons with key limes or other citrus fruits for endless variations on this recipe.

To start making the meringue, simmer the bean liquid in a saucepan until reduced by about half, 5 – 6 minutes. Place in a glass bowl and chill completely.

To make the pastry, combine the flour, sugar and salt in a large bowl. Cut in the cubed butter with a pastry blender until a crumb-like texture is formed with small pea-sized pieces of butter throughout. Create a well in the centre of the mixture and pour in the water. I fill a cup with ice and water to ensure that the water is very cold. Just make sure you don't get ice cubes in the pastry. Fold the pastry together a few times with a spatula until just mixed but still crumbly. Do not overmix!

Portion half of the pastry on a large piece of plastic film. Lift the sides of the plastic over the pastry to bring it together and gently form a ball. Finish wrapping the plastic and gently flatten into a thick disc. Do the same with the other half. Chill the pastry for at least 15 minutes before rolling out. You can also leave it up to 24 hours in the fridge, but it may need to stand at room temperature for 5 minutes to soften slightly before rolling out.

Preheat the oven to 220°C/425°F/Gas Mark 7 when ready to roll out the dough. Have ready 2 muffin tins or 18 mini foil tart tins. If you don't have 2 muffin tins then bake the cases in 2 batches, but chill the extra dough and only roll and cut out rounds once the first batch is complete.

CONTINUED

Flour the work surface, your hands, and a rolling pin and roll out one portion of the pastry to 3 – 4.75 mm/⅛ inch thick, stopping every couple of rolls to make sure the pastry isn't sticking. Gently lift the pastry and lightly flour underneath as you go.

Using a 10 cm/4 inch round cutter, cut out as many rounds as you can. Gently press the excess dough together and roll out again to cut out more rounds. Place each round into a muffin hole or tart tin and gently press into the base and sides. Pierce the pastry with a fork. Freeze for 15 minutes.

Bake for 18 – 20 minutes until golden brown and flaky. Remove from the oven and place on a wire rack to cool. Once cooled remove the pastry cases from the tin by gently nudging the edge with a knife or spatula. Place on a baking sheet or large plate. Continue your second batch of pastry cases if you only have one muffin tin.

Meanwhile, to prepare the filling, combine all the ingredients in a blender and blend until very smooth. Pour into a saucepan and cook over a medium heat, whisking constantly, for 5 – 6 minutes until thickened. Leave the filling to stand for 5 – 10 minutes, so it's not piping hot, but don't let it cool too much or it will gel up and be a little tricky to pour.

Fill the pastry cases with the filling and chill for at least 4 hours. The filling should be more firm and sticky to touch.

To finish the meringue, beat the chilled bean liquid with a hand mixer or in a stand mixer for 2 – 3 minutes until it looks foamy. Add the vanilla extract and cream of tartar and continue beating until stiff peaks form, 3 – 4 more minutes. Add 1 tablespoon of the icing sugar at a time while beating for a further 3 – 4 minutes. Add the xanthan gum last and beat for another 1 – 2 minutes. You'll notice that the meringue will become stiffer and slightly stickier after adding the xanthan gum.

Transfer the meringue to a piping bag with a large star nozzle or to a large ziplock bag with a small piece of the corner snipped off. Pipe a little swirl of meringue on top of each chilled tart. You can also dollop the meringue however you like on top.

Set the oven to grill and place the baking sheet with the tarts under the grill once hot. Hold the sheet with an oven glove and move it around under the grill to brown the tops as evenly as possible. The tarts will brown almost immediately, and they burn very quickly, so do not leave them unattended. Serve immediately. Chill leftovers for up to 1 week.

hot tip Whenever you open a can of beans, reserve the liquid, measure it, put it in a jar, label the jar with the amount, and freeze for later use.

This recipe makes enough filling and crust for a whole pie instead of tarts, but if you want to pile the meringue quite high, double the recipe for that.

raspberry funfetti pop tarts

MAKES 8 tarts
PREP TIME 1 hour
COOK TIME 30 – 35 minutes

rasberry filling

240 g/8½ oz fresh or frozen raspberries

200 g/7 oz granulated sugar

2 tablespoons freshly squeezed lemon juice

pastry

260 g/9 oz plain flour

1 tablespoon sugar

½ teaspoon salt

225 g/8 oz cold vegan butter, cubed

125 ml/4 fl oz ice-cold water

raspberry frosting

140 g/5 oz icing sugar

1½ tablespoons unsweetened non-dairy milk

1 tablespoon sprinkles of choice or desiccated coconut, to decourate

If I could travel back in time to my childhood the one thing I would want to change is being allowed to eat convenience breakfast pastries. I just recall all the delectable, mind-altering commercials featuring some kid eating a colourful rectangle of sugar and sprinkles. I remember I also just glared with envy at everyone at school eating them at lunch and recess. My parents wouldn't dare let me eat that crap! And I never ever did, not ever, even as an adult. But this cute homemade version uses the same pastry as the Classic Apple Pie (page 192) and Lemon Meringue Pie Tarts (page 197), and I've got to believe they taste about a million times better than those things that come wrapped in foil. Here's an ode to someone else's youth!

To make the filling, combine all the ingredients together in a large saucepan over a medium heat. Bring to a simmer. Once the filling is bubbling, lower the heat and simmer for 10 minutes until slightly thicker like jam.

Strain out the seeds by pouring the mixture through a sieve over another saucepan. Push the mixture back and forth with a spatula to allow a lot of thick jam to strain through the small holes. Simmer for 5 minutes. Turn off the heat and leave to cool completely at room temperature. The filling will thicken much more as it cools. Reserve 1 teaspoon of the filling to use in the icing.

To make the pastry, combine the flour, sugar and salt in a large bowl. Cut in the cubed butter with a pastry blender until a crumb-like texture is formed with small pea-sized pieces of butter throughout. Create a well in the centre of the mixture and pour in the water. Fold the pastry together a few times with a spatula until just mixed but still crumbly. Do not overmix!

Portion half of the pastry on a large piece of plastic film. Lift the sides of the plastic over the pastry to bring it together and gently form a ball. Finish wrapping the pastry in the plastic and gently flatten into a thick disc. Do the same with the other half. Chill the pastry for least 15 minutes before rolling out. You can also leave it up to 24 hours in the fridge, but it may need to stand at room temperature for 5 minutes to soften slightly before rolling out.

CONTINUED

Preheat the oven to 220°C/425°F/Gas Mark 7. Line 2 baking sheets with non-stick baking paper.

Flour the work surface, your hands and a rolling pin. Roll out one portion of the pastry 3 mm/⅛ inch thick and into a rectangle 40 – 43 cm/ 16 – 17 inches long by 15 – 18 cm/6 – 7 inches wide, stopping every couple of rolls to make sure the pastry isn't sticking. Gently lift the pastry and lightly flour underneath as you go.

Trim the edges slightly so you have an even rectangle shape. Cut the rectangle in half lengthways and then crossways into 4 pieces. You will have 8 rectangles approximately 10 cm/4 inches by 7.5 – 8 cm/ 3 – 3½ inches.

Spoon a large tablespoon of the raspberry filling on 4 rectangles. Take a bit of water on a finger and dab the edges of each rectangle. Top with a rectangle of pastry and gently press the edges together from the filling outwards to the edges. Use the tines of a fork to seal the edges all around. Place the tarts on 1 baking sheet and freeze for at least 15 minutes. Do the same method with the other portion of pastry and place the tarts on another sheet. Bake the frozen tarts first and freeze the second batch for at least 15 minutes.

Bake for 15 – 18 minutes until the tarts are golden brown. Remove the tarts from the baking sheet to a wire rack and leave to cool completely before icing.

To make the icing, combine the reserved 1 teaspoon raspberry filling with the sugar and non-dairy milk in a bowl and mix until smooth.

Spoon some of the icing over each tart and spread across the centre. The icing should drape nicely over the top but still leave the edges of the tart exposed. If the icing is too thin, add a bit more sugar; if it's too thick to spread, add a bit more non-dairy milk. While the icing is still wet, add the sprinkles or coconut. Allow the tarts to dry completely before storing between layers of non-stick baking paper in a container at room temperature. They are best consumed the same day as baking. A day later, you might want to warm them slightly before eating.

get saucy

Oh yes, I'm a sauce superfan. . . but really, who isn't! Food is nothing without sauces or condiments, and you're more than ready to sauce up your meals with all these ideas. These pages are inevitably going to get splattered and dirty because you'll be referencing them with pretty much every recipe in the book. I advise keeping your faves on hand all the time so you're ready to drizzle, dip, douse and drown all your cravings!

The nacho cheese

MAKES about 350 g/12 oz
PREP TIME 20 minutes
COOK TIME 10 minutes

ingredients

1 small peeled, cubed white potato (about 140 g/5 oz)

1 peeled, diced carrot (about 60 g/2¼ oz)

4 tablespoons vegetable oil

4 tablespoons non-dairy milk or water

1 tablespoon nutritional yeast

1½ teaspoons arrowroot flour

1 teaspoon garlic powder

1 teaspoon onion powder

½ teaspoon sea salt

2 teaspoons freshly squeezed lemon juice

6 pickled jalapeño slices or to taste, plus 3 tablespoons brine

1 tablespoon tomato purée

If The Nacho Cheese were an album, it would be Dr Dre's *The Chronic*. Not only is it gonna make you feel nostalgic for that ooey gooey sauce you get at the cinema or carnivals, but it's also gonna be on repeat in your kitchen! You don't need to feel bad about it either because your new favourite cheese sauce is made from potatoes and carrots. No, that's not a typo. . . it's your mantra.

Bring a pot of water to the boil and cook the potato and carrot until fork-tender, 6 – 8 minutes. Drain the vegetables and immediately place in a high-powdered blender. If you cook the potatoes too long, they will become starchy and your sauce will not be smooth.

Add the remaining ingredients to the blender and combine on high until smooth. Your sauce may be hot enough to serve immediately from the blender. If not, heat it in a saucepan for a few minutes until just bubbling and warm or reheat in a microwave.

When you reheat the sauce, a small amount of non-dairy milk or water may be required to get a smooth consistency again.

hot tip This is so good you could make more than you need and freeze it in portions. Can be frozen for up to 1 month. It keeps and reheats very well!

For those nights when you want mac & cheese (page 131) but you're thinking 'ain't nobody got time for that,' just make a batch of The Nacho Cheese and boil some mac. . . there, done! You could add anything else you want to this easy mac & cheese like broccoli, green peas, sautéed onions or vegan beef-style ground mince (such as Quorn). Also, if you're nut-free, this is your mac!

the parm

MAKES abou 75 g/6 oz
PREP TIME 10 minutes

ingredients

- 80 g/3 oz raw cashews, almonds, or pistachios
- 12 g/⅓ oz nutritional yeast
- 1 teaspoon sea salt

Remember at university (maybe even now in adulthood) when you would always have a big shaker of Parmesan in your fridge that never seemed to go bad? We have the perfect replacement that you'll be shaking on everything. And it's made from only three simple ingredients. For a slightly different flavour, you can use salted roasted nuts – just reduce the amount of salt you add afterwards.

Combine all the ingredients together in a food processor and process until a fine crumb or flour is formed.

Store in a jar or container in the fridge for up to 3 weeks.

hot tip In a pinch you can make a half batch of The Parm in a coffee grinder. Be sure to clean it thoroughly beforehand!

the tartar sauce

MAKES about 225 ml/8 fl oz
PREP TIME 20 minutes

ingredients

- 227 g/8 oz vegan mayonnaise
- 45 g/1¾ oz finely chopped gherkin and 2 teaspoons gherkin brine
- 1 teaspoon garlic powder
- 1 tablespoon freshly squeezed lemon juice
- ⅛ teaspoon ground pepper

There's not much to say or divulge about tartar sauce. It's dang good and it's not hiding any secrets because it's basically just gherkins and mayo. I mean, if you're really lazy just combine those two things and call it a day. But in the hot for food kitchen we keep things fancy AF, so here's the real deal that's slathered on the Filet-O-Tempeh Sandwich (page 100).

Combine all the ingredients in a bowl or jar and chill until using. Consume within 7 days.

The mozza

MAKES about 300 g/10½ oz
PREP TIME 30 minutes
COOK TIME 10 minutes

ingredients

60 g/2¼ oz raw cashews, soaked in hot water for 20 minutes

225 ml/8 fl oz unsweetened non-dairy milk

1 tablespoon tapioca flour

1 teaspoon nutritional yeast

½ – 1 teaspoon sea salt

½ teaspoon garlic powder

¼ teaspoon onion powder

¼ teaspoon ground white pepper

2 teaspoons freshly squeezed lemon juice

I'm not going to lie. Mozzarella is very hard to re-create in plant-based form, especially in the home kitchen. So truthfully, this is more of a mozza sauce. It doesn't have that über-stringy texture, but the flavour and mind trickery are all there. Expect a thick and gooey version that's creamy, salty and just tangy enough to peek through many savoury dishes. It'll brown up when baked on top of a margherita pizza or a crusty crouton for Gooey French Onion Soup (page 79), or when drizzled on Butternut Squash Cannelloni (page 127). In some of our recipes, you can swap arrowroot or cornflour for the tapioca, but tapioca creates the best texture for this particular recipe so I wouldn't deviate!

Drain and rinse the cashews. Place in a high-powered blender with the remaining ingredients and combine until very smooth. Start with ½ teaspoon of the salt and adjust to your taste after the sauce is heated in the next step.

Heat the sauce in a small saucepan over a medium heat, whisking constantly, until just thickened, 8 – 10 minutes.

You'll use all the mozza in the recipes noted above, but if you have leftovers, chill for up to 1 week. Before using the sauce, you might need to add a little more non-dairy milk or water while reheating to smooth it out, or try blending the sauce again.

hot tip You can soak cashews for up to 7 days in the fridge so they're always ready to go! Just be sure to change the water every couple of days. Don't forget, my measurements are always the presoaked amount!

the bbq sauce

MAKES 300 ml/10 fl oz
PREP TIME 10 minutes
COOK TIME 55 minutes

ingredients

200 g/7 oz brown sugar

475 ml/16 fl oz water

475 ml/16 fl oz apple cider vinegar

115 g/4 oz tomato purée

2 tablespoons molasses

1 teaspoon mustard powder or Dijon mustard

1 teaspoon smoked paprika

1 teaspoon sea salt

1 teaspoon garlic powder

1 teaspoon onion powder

½ teaspoon ground pepper

I can certainly empathize with the desire to buy a shop-bought BBQ sauce. I do it all the time too. . . because of laziness! But not everything on the shelf is vegan friendly. Be on the look-out for anchovies, regular Worcestershire sauce, honey and of course 'natural flavors' that aren't always plant based either. You may or may not be concerned about that, but in the end it's worth the extra time to DIY. Your recipes will taste more authentic, comforting and real.

Whisk all the ingredients together in a saucepan.

Bring to a low boil. Reduce the heat and simmer, stirring occasionally, for 40 – 45 minutes until thickened.

Leave to cool completely before storing in the fridge. Consume within 2 weeks.

The guac sauce

MAKES about 475 ml/16 fl oz
PREP TIME 20 minutes

ingredients

2 ripe avocados, stoned and peeled

125 ml/4 fl oz full-fat coconut milk

4 tablespoons freshly squeezed lime juice

1 teaspoon hot sauce

¼ teaspoon garlic powder

¼ teaspoon onion powder

¼ teaspoon sea salt

¼ teaspoon ground pepper

I'm all for a chunky guac, but this sauce is just so smooth and suave you'll want to introduce it to everyone! It is meant to be drizzled and dippable. I've got it smothered on the Spicy Black Bean Taquitos (page 50). You can also put it all over tacos or try it as a dip for fries.

Place all the ingredients in a high-powered blender and blend until very smooth. If your coconut milk has separated in the can, make sure the milk and cream are combined before measuring the milk and adding to the blender.

Chill the sauce and consume within 2 – 3 days.

The soured cream

MAKES about 225 ml/8 fl oz
PREP TIME 25 minutes

ingredients

120 g/4¼ oz raw cashews, soaked in hot water for 20 minutes

125 ml/4 fl oz unsweetened non-dairy milk or water

2 tablespoons freshly squeezed lemon juice

½ teaspoon apple cider vinegar

½ teaspoon onion powder

½ teaspoon garlic powder

¼ teaspoon sea salt

¼ teaspoon ground white pepper

I put this on everything! So don't be a sceptic. This creamy cashew soured cream does the trick to replace soured cream in your plant-based life. It even works well as a base for other sauces, so if you have a little leftover, repurpose it into something new and delicious. Did somebody say cashew-based ranch or creamy French dressing? No, just me hearing voices again?

Drain and rinse the cashews and place in a high-powered blender with the remaining ingredients. Combine on high until very smooth.

Chill for at least 1 hour before serving. The soured cream keeps for up to 7 days in the fridge. I would make and consume this as soon as possible for a fresh taste. This isn't the best recipe to freeze and keep for longer storage.

The maple-mustard dip

MAKES 90 ml/3 fl oz
PREP TIME 10 minutes

ingredients

60 g/2¼ oz Dijon mustard or grainy mustard

1 tablespoon yellow mustard

1 tablespoon vegan mayonnaise

1 – 2 tablespoons maple syrup, to taste

This sweet and tangy dip is your substitute for honey mustard, so get dippin' all your faves like vegan chicken fingers, pretzels, onion rings and the Herb-loaded Sausage Rolls (page 37), or use it as a sandwich spread. Listen, I'm not going to tell you how to live your life, but just use it when you need a little sweetness to balance things out!

Combine all the ingredients together in a bowl or jar. Chill until serving. Consume within 3 weeks.

the red pepper relish

MAKES 225 ml/8 fl oz
PREP TIME 20 minutes
COOK TIME 20 minutes

ingredients

2 finely chopped red bell pepper (about 220 g/7¾ oz)

1 finely chopped onion (about 115 g/4 oz)

2 tablespoons olive oil

5 – 6 garlic cloves, very finely chopped

1 teaspoon sea salt

½ teaspoon red pepper flakes

1 teaspoon Dijon mustard or mustard powder

100 g/3½ oz sugar

125 ml/4 fl oz white wine vinegar

This relish is divine with the Mushroom & Leek Quiche (page 22), but you could also use it in place of a hot sauce to pair with other brunch fare like The Big Brekky Pan (page 12) or The Best Breakfast Sandwich (page 16). It's even a tasty dip for the Herb-loaded Sausage Rolls (page 37).

Sauté the pepper and onion in the olive oil in a saucepan over a medium heat for 3 – 4 minutes until soft and fragrant.

Add the garlic, salt, chilli flakes and mustard and sauté, stirring frequently, for about 5 minutes, reducing the heat to medium-low so the garlic doesn't burn.

Add the sugar and vinegar, bring to a simmer and cook, stirring occasionally, for 10 minutes until most of the liquid is absorbed.

Leave to cool completely before storing in the fridge or serving over warm quiche. Consume within 7 days.

the spicy peanut sauce

MAKES about 225 ml/8 fl oz
PREP TIME 10 minutes

ingredients

125 ml/4 fl oz water

125 g/4½ oz smooth natural peanut butter

4 tablespoons low-salt soy sauce or tamari

2 tablespoons freshly squeezed lime juice

1 tablespoon plus 1 teaspoon sambal oelek (chilli paste) or Sriracha

2 teaspoons sugar or maple or agave syrup

Peanut butter, spice and everything nice! This is the simplest, easiest peanut sauce that you'll want for drowning noodles in over and over again. First peep the Spicy Peanut Noodles (page 121) and then start daydreaming about all the other things you could smother with it.

In a blender, combine all the ingredients together until very smooth or stir together in a jar. If stirring the sauce, you may need to use warm water to smooth out the peanut butter.

Use the sauce immediately or store in the fridge and consume within 7 days. You may need to add more warm water to smooth out the sauce before using in a recipe.

hot tip Switch this sauce up by substituting almond, cashew or sunflower butter for the peanut butter!

The red sauce & the rosé sauce

MAKES 1.4 litres/2½ pints
PREP TIME 25 minutes
COOK TIME 1 hour

The red sauce

2.3 kg/5 lb Roma tomatoes (18 to 20 tomatoes)

2 tablespoons olive oil

2 finely chopped onions (about 170 g/6 oz)

3 garlic cloves, very finely chopped

3 tablespoons tomato purée

1 bay leaf

1 teaspoon dried oregano

1 teaspoon sea salt

½ teaspoon ground pepper

24 g/1 oz fresh basil leaves

The rosé sauce

120 g/4¼ oz raw cashews, soaked in hot water for 20 minutes

225 ml/8 fl oz water

1.4 litres/2½ pints The Red Sauce

This homemade tomato sauce is so incredibly tasty, and canned tomatoes just don't do it justice. I tried and tested, but the sauce isn't the same. So if you can put in a little nonna-style hustle to make it right, you'll be in spaghetti heaven! The sauce is easy to customize by making it spicy with chilli flakes or by adding more basil or garlic to your liking. How about bringing a little vegan sausage to the party too? And for some extra richness, add cashew cream for a delectable rosé sauce (instructions follow).

To make the red sauce, cut the tomatoes in half lengthways and scoop out the seeds and excess watery flesh. This is easiest to do with your fingers by pressing an index finger and middle finger inside each tomato half and running them down the length of the tomato. The seeds should slide out. You don't have to get every single one, just the majority. Cut the tomatoes into a large dice.

Heat the olive oil in a large pot over a medium heat and add the onions. Sauté for 2 – 3 minutes until soft and fragrant. Add the garlic, tomato purée, bay leaf, oregano, salt and pepper. Sauté for 2 minutes.

Add the tomatoes. Tear the basil leaves by hand and add to the pot. Stir to combine and bring to a simmer. Continue to simmer for 15 minutes, uncovered, stirring occasionally.

Remove the bay leaf and set aside. Using an immersion blender, blend the sauce until mostly smooth, getting rid of the large tomato chunks. If you don't have an immersion blender, you can pour the sauce into a regular blender and pulse a few times to get it mostly smooth, then add it back to the pot. Return the bay leaf to the pot and continue to simmer the sauce for 25 – 30 minutes uncovered.

If making the rosé sauce, drain and rinse the cashews. Add to a high-powered blender with the water and blend until very smooth. Stir the cashew cream into the pot of red sauce during the last 10 minutes of simmering. Heat through and serve.

Allow the sauce to cool completely before storing in jars. It can be frozen for up to 3 months.

the hollandaise sauce

MAKES about 225 ml/8 fl oz
PREP TIME 15 minutes
COOK TIME 5 minutes

ingredients

40 g/1½ oz sliced blanched almonds

125 ml/4 fl oz unsweetened non-dairy milk

2 tablespoons nutritional yeast

½ teaspoon mustard powder

½ teaspoon sea salt

½ teaspoon ground white pepper

¼ teaspoon ground turmeric

2 tablespoons freshly squeezed lemon juice

1 tablespoon white wine vinegar

1 tablespoon vegetable oil

Have you ever Googled how to make real hollandaise? It's rich on rich on rich! Rather than relying on butter and egg yolks for fat and flavour, I make the base with lean, mean almonds. You're definitely serving it with the Tofu Benny (page 20), but it's also a classic pairing with grilled asparagus or other green veggies.

Place all the ingredients in a high-powered blender and blend until very smooth. If you need to thin the sauce, add small amounts of non-dairy milk until the desired consistency is achieved.

Heat the sauce over a low heat in a saucepan, whisking constantly, before serving. If you overheat the sauce or forget to whisk it constantly, it will thicken and get lumpy. If this occurs, re-blend it to smooth it out or add more non-dairy milk or water.

When reheating leftovers, you'll definitely need to add a bit more non-dairy milk or water to thin out the sauce again. It keeps up to 7 days in the fridge.

the gravy

MAKES about 475 ml/16 fl oz
PREP TIME 20 minutes
COOK TIME 10 minutes

ingredients

1 finely chopped small shallot (about 35 g/1¼ oz)

3 garlic cloves, very finely chopped

4 tablespoons vegan butter

1 teaspoon fresh thyme leaves, or ½ teaspoon dried thyme

1 teaspoon fresh rosemary, or ½ teaspoon dried rosemary

½ teaspoon ground nutmeg

½ teaspoon celery salt

150 g/5½ oz tahini

125 ml/4 fl oz low-salt tamari or soy sauce

75 g/2¾ oz maple syrup

4 tablespoons low-salt vegetable stock, or more if needed

2 tablespoons vegan Worcestershire sauce

All the best food is brown. Have you heard that one before? It's true. . . it's a hashtag! This gravy wins best in show for its performance in Waffle-topped Cottage Pie (page 159) and for smothering the Bangers & Mash (page 161). But feel free to skip the main dishes and drink it directly from the gravy boat when no one is looking. We won't tell!

In a saucepan, sauté the shallot and garlic in the vegan butter for 2 minutes.

Add the thyme, rosemary, nutmeg and celery salt and sauté for 1 – 2 more minutes.

Stir in the tahini, tamari, maple syrup, 4 tablespoons of stock, and Worcestershire sauce and simmer over a low heat for 3 – 4 minutes. Add more stock as necessary to thin out the gravy to your desired consistency.

Allow the gravy to cool completely before storing or freezing. It will keep in the fridge for up to 2 weeks or in the freezer for up to 3 months. When reheating the gravy, add more water or vegetable stock to thin it to your desired consistency. The gravy will not become bland from diluting.

the caesar dressing

MAKES about 475 ml/16 fl oz
PREP TIME 30 minutes
COOK TIME 35 minutes

ingredients

- 1 garlic bulb
- 1 tablespoon olive oil
- 2 pinches of sea salt
- 90 g/3¼ oz raw cashews, soaked in hot water for 20 minutes
- 175 ml/6 fl oz water
- 1 pitted Medjool date
- 3½ tablespoons nutritional yeast
- 1 teaspoon sea salt
- 1 teaspoon ground pepper
- 1 teaspoon grated lemon zest and 3 tablespoons lemon juice
- 1 tablespoon apple cider vinegar
- ½ teaspoon Dijon mustard

This dressing has been on the blog since inception and continues to be one of the favourite things I've made. Don't mess with it – it's perfect! If you've never roasted garlic, don't be intimidated. It's easy to do, and the smooth flavour and aroma are what makes this dressing something special.

Preheat the oven to 200°C/400°F/Gas Mark 6.

Peel the outer layers from the garlic bulb, leaving a thin layer intact. Cut the bulb in half crossways to expose the cloves. Coat the cloves with the olive oil and sprinkle each half with a pinch of salt. Place in a small baking tin and roast for 35 minutes until the cloves are browned and soft to touch.

Remove the roasted cloves from the bulb with a fork and place in a high-powered blender.

Drain and rinse the soaked cashews. Place the cashews and the remaining ingredients in the blender and combine on high until very smooth.

The dressing will be slightly warm from the roasted garlic and can be served immediately on the Brussels Sprouts Caesar Salad (page 63). Store in the fridge and consume within 7 days.

hot tip Nut-free folks can substitute crumbled soft tofu for the cashews.

three easy dressings

One very important piece of advice for loving yourself is never buy a pre-made dip or salad dressing if you can help it! It's a big waste of money, and these products are full of weird ingredients you can't pronounce. Also, it's not so easy to find creamy dressings that are both vegan and delicious, so just make them yourself. This is the holy trinity of dressings and dips: The Classic Ranch, The Thousand Island and The Creamy Cucumber. They're my saviours when I want to make salad into a comfort food affair and less reminiscent of rabbit food. But they're not just for salad. You'll find them used as sandwich spreads and dips throughout the book. Get in the game and dog-ear this page!

MAKES about 225 ml/8 fl oz
PREP TIME 20 minutes

the classic ranch

ingredients

- 227 g/8 oz vegan mayonnaise
- 1 tablespoon finely chopped fresh dill
- 1 tablespoon finely chopped fresh flat-leaf parsley
- 1 tablespoon finely chopped chives
- 2 teaspoons apple cider vinegar
- 1 teaspoon onion powder
- ¼ teaspoon sea salt
- ¼ teaspoon ground pepper

Stir all the ingredients together in a bowl until well combined.

Store in the fridge for up to 10 days.

The Thousand island

ingredients

- 227 g/8 oz vegan mayonnaise
- 4 tablespoons sweet green relish
- 2 tablespoons ketchup
- 1 tablespoon apple cider vinegar
- 1 tablespoon sambal oelek (chilli paste) or hot sauce
- 1 teaspoon onion powder
- 2 tablespoons finely chopped chives
- ¼ teaspoon sea salt
- ¼ teaspoon ground pepper

Stir all the ingredients together in a bowl until well combined.

Store in the fridge for up to 10 days.

hot tip Fresh herbs create a more authentic taste and are preferred, but in a pinch you can use dried. I don't know you, but maybe you like your dip thick and your salad dressing thinned out. Whatever your pleasure just add a tablespoon or two of water or non-dairy milk to these 3 recipes once they're made to achieve your desired consistency!

the creamy cucumber

ingredients

- ⅓ cucumber
- 227 g/8 oz vegan mayonnaise
- 2 tablespoons freshly squeezed lemon juice
- 2 garlic cloves
- 2 teaspoons apple cider vinegar
- 1 teaspoon finely chopped fresh dill
- ¼ teaspoon sea salt
- ¼ teaspoon ground pepper

Grate the cucumber. Place in a sieve, nut milk bag or double layer of muslin and squeeze out the excess water.

Place the cucumber and the remaining ingredients in a high-powered blender and blend until very smooth. You can also combine all the ingredients in a jar, but be sure to very finely chop the garlic and chop the grated cucumber. This will result in a chunkier consistency.

Store in the fridge for up to 10 days. Some of the water from the cucumber may separate. You can shake the dressing to combine again.

the aiolis

Meet The Aiolis! Your friendly neighbourhood family you'll want to get to know very well. There's something for everyone here: sun-dried tomato, roasted garlic, spicy Sriracha, jalapeño-lime and horseradish-dill. You'll find these used heavily throughout the book, but my hope is that soon enough you'll be such an aioli pro that you'll be able to whip up your own flavourful concoctions in a flash! If you can make your own homemade mayo, do so. It will save you all kinds of money! But it's essential to have an immersion or high-powered blender since it's the only way the oil and liquid can emulsify to get the right texture. If you don't have either, you'll have to make the investment in pre-made vegan mayonnaise, and thankfully there's a ton of products on the market now. What a time to be alive! The mayo and aiolis should be chilled and consumed within 2 weeks.

MAKES about 300 g/10½ oz
PREP TIME 10 minutes

homemade vegan mayo

ingredients

125 ml/4 fl oz unsweetened non-dairy milk

½ teaspoon sea salt

2 teaspoons apple cider vinegar

1 teaspoon mustard powder
or Dijon mustard

225 ml/8 fl oz vegetable oil
(sunflower or rapeseed are best)

If using a blender, place all the ingredients except the oil in a high-powered blender. Start blending on low while you slowly drizzle in the oil, and then increase the speed until the mayo is thick and fluffy.

If using an immersion blender, place all the ingredients in a tall jar or tall plastic container. Submerge the blender, then turn it on and blend until the mayo is thick and fluffy.

MAKES about 150 g/5½ oz
PREP TIME 15 minutes

the sundried tomato aioli

ingredients

15 g/½ oz dried sundried tomatoes

115 g/4 oz vegan mayonnaise

2 tablespoons freshly squeezed lemon juice

¼ teaspoon chilli powder

¼ teaspoon mustard powder
or Dijon mustard

¼ teaspoon sea salt

¼ teaspoon ground pepper

Soak the sun-dried tomatoes in warm water for 10 minutes and then drain. This helps to soften the tomatoes for blending.

Add the sun-dried tomatoes and remaining ingredients to a high-powered blender and blend until very smooth. Alternatively, use an immersion blender to combine all the ingredients in a tall jar or other container and blend until very smooth.

MAKES about 150 g/5½ oz
PREP TIME 15 minutes

the horseradish-dill aioli

ingredients

150 g/5½ oz vegan mayonnaise

1 tablespoon vegan horseradish

1 tablespoon freshly squeezed lemon juice

1 tablespoon finely chopped fresh dill

¼ teaspoon ground pepper

Stir all the ingredients together in a bowl until well combined.

MAKES about 150 g/5½ oz
PREP TIME 15 minutes
COOK TIME 35 minutes

the roasted garlic aioli

ingredients

1 garlic bulb

1 tablespoon olive oil

Sea salt

150 g/5½ oz vegan mayonnaise

1 tablespoon freshly squeezed lemon juice

¼ teaspoon salt

⅛ teaspoon ground pepper

⅛ teaspoon cayenne pepper

½ teaspoon vegan Worcestershire sauce

Preheat the oven to 200°C/400°F/Gas Mark 6.

To roast the garlic, peel any excess layers from the bulb, leaving some skin intact. Cut the bulb in half crossways to expose the cloves. Coat the cloves with the olive oil and sprinkle each half with a pinch of sea salt. Place in a small baking tin and roast for 35 minutes until the cloves are browned and soft to the touch.

Remove the roasted cloves from the bulb with a fork and place in a high-powered blender. Add the remaining ingredients and combine on high until smooth. Alternatively, use an immersion blender to blend the roasted cloves and remaining ingredients in a tall jar or other container until very smooth.

MAKES about 300 g/10½ oz
PREP TIME 15 minutes

the jalapeño-lime aioli

ingredients

227 g/8 oz vegan mayonnaise

35 g/1¼ oz pickled jalapeño slices, drained

Grated zest and juice of 1 lime

¼ teaspoon chili powder

¼ teaspoon sea salt

Place all the ingredients in a high-powered blender and combine on high until smooth. Alternatively, use an immersion blender to combine all the ingredients in a tall jar or other container until very smooth.

MAKES about 150 g/5½ oz
PREP TIME 10 minutes

the spicy sriracha aioli

ingredients

150 g/5½ oz vegan mayonnaise

2 tablespoons Sriracha sauce

1 tablespoon freshly squeezed lime juice

Stir all the ingredients together in a bowl until well combined.

acknowledgements

Thank you to YOU. . . for buying this book and using it as a tool for spreading more vegan love. I hope it brings you much inspiration. Share it, love it and go vegan (if you're not already)!

Thank you the MOST to John. This book wouldn't exist without you. Thank you for always making me laugh and squashing my inner sabotage. I love you, forever.

Thank you to my amazing group of recipe testers: Joseph Rapuano, Bianca Migueles, Laura Takahashi, Zachary Smith, Erin Yantha, Kendra Korinetz, Samantha Antille, Becky Hughes, Veronique Daoust, Kaja Köhnle, Nolwenn Petitbois and Jon Lubanski.

Thank you to JBC, Nat, Lo and all the Peace Warriors for helping me through my mental blocks surrounding this cookbook. Your strength and inspiration keep me going!

Thank you to my parents, Richard and Jackie, for always giving me the freedom to make my own choices and letting me follow my dreams.

Thank you to Rick, Ashley, Aimee, Maureen, Morgan, Myia and all the stars at Kin Community for working so hard and believing in hot for food. This book certainly wouldn't exist had we not connected. Rick, thank you for daring us to give YouTube a real shot. You turned a sceptic into a CEO!

Thank you to Tiffany Astle and the penelopePR team for being great friends and colleagues. You've been so good to me and you helped the hot for food dream become a reality.

Thank you to Sally Ekus. It was divine timing that you emailed me and I'm so grateful you're part of the team. You are a powerhouse! Here's to many more endeavours together!

Thank you to Kelly, Emma, Margaux, Lisa R, Lisa F, and all the amazing women at Ten Speed Press who have helped make this book a reality. You are all incredible! Girl power!

Thank you to Andrea Magyar at Penguin Random House for being authentic, honest and generous. You helped me realize that making a cookbook was the right thing to do for my heart and soul.

Thank you to Magda Zofia and Vanessa Heins for all the hard work and creativity you devoted to the photography in this cookbook.

Thanks, Snickles, for not helping at all with this book but for always being around when I need a cuddle! Sorry for forcing you into photo shoots. . . forgive me!

—xo lauren

index

10 9 8 7 6 5 4 3 2 1

Ebury Press, an imprint of Ebury Publishing,
20 Vauxhall Bridge Road, London, SW1V 2SA

Ebury Press is part of the Penguin Random House group
of companies whose addresses can be found at global.
penguinrandomhouse.com

Penguin
Random House
UK

First published by Ebury Press in 2018
Originally published in the USA by Ten Speed Press

OVEN TEMPERTURES
All celcius oven temperatures are for conventional ovens. For
fan-assisted ovens decrease the temperature by 20 degrees.

www.penguin.co.uk

A CIP catalogue record for this book is available from the British
Library

Design: Margaux Keres and Lisa Ferkel

ISBN: 9781785039386

Printed and bound in Italy by L.E.G.O. S.p.A

Penguin Random House is committed to a sustainable future for
our business, our readers and our planet. This book is made from
Forest Stewardship Council® certified paper.